Letter Writing
Made Easy

Publications International, Ltd.

Cover image: Shutterstock.com

Author: Erika Swanson Geiss

Contributing writer: Lisa Brooks

Louis Weber, CEO
Publications International, Ltd.
7373 North Cicero Avenue
Lincolnwood, Illinois 60712

ISBN: 978-1-4508-8229-3

Manufactured in U.S.A.

8 7 6 5 4 3 2 1

❧ Contents ❧

Finding the Right Words   4-6

Chapter 1: The Basics   7-22

Chapter 2: Saying Thank You   23-45

Chapter 3: Invitations   46-66

Chapter 4: Acceptance and Regret   67-71

Chapter 5: Congratulations   72-80

Chapter 6: Get Well Soon   81-82

Chapter 7: Sending Sympathy   83-91

Chapter 8: I Love You...Or Maybe Not   92-97

Chapter 9: Writing While On Vacation   98-99

Chapter 10: The Holiday Letter   100-107

Chapter 11: Thinking of You   108-112

Chapter 12: Anger and Apologies   113-121

Chapter 13: It's All Business   122-141

Chapter 14: School Time   142-157

Chapter 15: Organizations   158-169

Chapter 16: Letters of Recommendation   170-177

Chapter 17: E-mail   178-185

Chapter 18: Texting and Social Media   186-192

Finding the Right Words

Everyone loves to receive letters in the mail. Thank-you notes, postcards from exotic locations, or just random "thinking of you" notes from good friends are all instant day-brighteners. But too often, our mailboxes are full of the cookie-cutter mass mailings found in every box in the neighborhood—bills, catalogs, and advertisements. Some days, the entire contents of the mailbox are relegated directly to the recycling bin. So it's always a fun surprise to open the mailbox door and see an envelope with telltale human handwriting, and know that someone has taken the time to put their thoughts to paper just for you.

But when it comes to actually *writing* one of those letters, the task can seem daunting. Even when we know that sending a letter is the proper thing to do, it can be difficult to get started. We sit down with every intention of writing; but distractions block our creativity and looming chores take precedence over communication. Often, finding the right words for each specific occasion can be overwhelming.

In an age when nearly every household has at least one computer, the majority of our written correspondence now consists of e-mails, text messages, and social media postings. But when you get right down to the details of communication—spelling, grammar, punctuation, tone of voice—what is the difference between old-school handwritten letters and our new, electronic forms of correspondence? Very simply, there is no difference. Or rather, there should be no difference. The same rules we apply to written letters can be applied to any form of written correspondence. Our communication has not changed; rather, it has evolved.

But even with all of our technology, handwritten letters are still a necessary reality. Some people don't use e-mail or social media; and even many of those who do still consider written letters to be more professional or polite, depending on the circumstance. Consider the time and thought that goes into choosing a gift for someone, for instance—would you rather they send a brief text message or e-mail as a thank you, or would you rather receive a handwritten note, knowing that they also put time and thought into their thank you?

Most of us probably appreciate the effort that goes into writing a handwritten letter, but we still find it difficult to sit down and write one ourselves. What's more, while most of us also make use of electronic communication on a daily basis, we often fall into the trap of believing we can be less conscientious with our words. E-mails, Facebook postings, and text messages end up looking like unimportant after-thoughts, and we force the reader to decipher sloppy text.

So essentially we have two communication problems: We struggle with handwritten letters as well as electronic correspondence. That's where *Letter Writing Made Easy* comes in. In this book, you'll find plenty of examples and tips to make any kind of communication easier, whether handwritten or typed into your computer or smart phone.

Do you struggle to find the right words for certain occasions? Does your stationery sit before you, blank and neglected, as you search for ideas? This book will provide you with inspiration for writing thank-you notes, sympathy letters, business letters, love letters, and more. Do you draw a blank when composing e-mails to contractors, or wonder whether you should post about certain aspects of your life on your Facebook page? *Letter Writing Made Easy* will show you how simple it is for your e-mails to look polished and professional, and it will help you navigate the sometimes confusing road of social media.

Writing letters doesn't have to be difficult or frustrating. And electronic communication can be a wonderful tool, not only for your personal enjoyment, but for your professional life, as well. Let *Letter Writing Made Easy* be your guide when you have communication concerns or when you're drawing a blank. With this book, you'll always be prepared to share the right words at the right time.

❋ Chapter 1 ❋
The Basics

Before we get into the nitty-gritty of different types of letters, let's start with some simple guidelines. We'll break down the parts of a letter, discuss some tips that apply to many kinds of letters, and talk about preparing your correspondence to send.

THE ANATOMY OF A LETTER

Like the human body, a car, or a computer, a letter has different parts to it, each with its own function, arrangement, and purpose. A letter is composed of ten basic parts with an optional eleventh part. The parts of a letter are:

* ❋ Heading/return address
* ❋ Date
* ❋ Addressee's name (also called the inside address)
* ❋ Addressee's address
* ❋ Salutation
* ❋ Body
* ❋ Closing
* ❋ Complimentary closing
* ❋ Hand-signed signature
* ❋ Typed or printed signature
* ❋ Postscript

Letters also come in several styles, but each has the same basic parts. The various letter styles are block, semi-block, and simple formats, each of which is left justified. That is, the left margin is flush, meaning all paragraphs align with the left margin. Letters should be single-spaced between lines and double-spaced between paragraphs. Allow space for your hand-signed signature.

Block Format

Here is an example of block format:

Paul Haynes
35 Winding Road
Sodona, AZ 86336

July 19, 2014

Michelle Pesci
6570 Cactus Blossom Trail
Sodona, AZ 86336

Dear Michelle,

I want to thank you and John for your generous hospitality while our house was being renovated. Alexis and I don't know where to begin with our gratitude and hope that the extended stay wasn't too much of an inconvenience. Please know that our home is always open to you, and we hope that you and the kids will be able to come to our housewarming next month.

Very sincerely yours,

Paul

Paul

Semi-Block Format

With the same letter, here is an example of semi-block format.

Paul Haynes
35 Winding Road
Sodona, AZ 86336

July 19, 2014

Michelle Pesci
6570 Cactus Blossom Trail
Sodona, AZ 86336

Dear Michelle,

    I want to thank you and John for your generous hospitality while our house was being renovated. Alexis and I don't know where to begin with our gratitude and hope that the extended stay wasn't too much of an inconvenience. Please know that our home is always open to you, and we hope that you and the kids will be able to come to our housewarming next month.

                              Very sincerely yours,

                              Paul

                              Paul

You will notice that in the semi-block format, the paragraph is indented and the complimentary closing and signature parts are placed to the right, rather than left justified, as they are in the block-letter format.

Simple Format

The simple format follows the same conventions as the block-letter format and does not contain the salutation or the formal closing parts.

G.F. Basil and Sons
2789 West Boulevard
Sodona, AZ 86336

July 19, 2014

Michelle Pesci
6570 Cactus Blossom Trail
Sodona, AZ 86336

Rate Changes Effective September 1, 2014

This letter is to inform our valued customers that as of September 1, 2014, our rates will be increasing. Transportation rates will increase by 0.6 percent, and goods and services will be assessed an additional 0.4 percent tax, as stipulated by recent industry regulations.

G.F. Basil and Sons

TAKING ON THE TASK

Now that you have your tools and know your format, you can start writing. There are four steps to writing: plan, write, edit, and rewrite.

Plan Your Prose

Always start with a draft. Some like to compose their drafts on the computer, while others still prefer to write it out longhand on manuscript paper. Either way, writing a draft gives you a chance to get your ideas out on paper and then edit the work. Writing a draft is important because your letter, especially in a business situation, is the very first impression that you will make, so you want it to be stellar. For short, personal correspondence, you might want to skip the draft, but it is not recommended for two reasons. First, if the nature of the letter is serious or intense, it is wise to do a draft first so that you don't send something you might regret having in print later. Second, since you will be mailing the letter on your fine note stationery, you don't want to waste it with crossed out words and other edits.

Keep It Simple

In some situations, the urge is great to write long, lofty sentences worthy of being compared to Charles Dickens. But take a tip from Hemingway and write short, simple sentences. You're not writing the next Great American Novel, you're writing a letter, which means that you've got to make your point and make it quickly. Your job is to give your reader enough information and make it fluid enough so that they want to read on, and if enclosures are included, read those, too. You will occasionally need to pull out the thesaurus and use words that would make your elementary school English teacher proud. But use such words with caution and only when you need to make a decided impact on your reader.

Know Your Audience

Drafts allow you to tailor your letter to the person who will be reading it. In other words, you need to consider your audience. Just as you would address your best friend differently than your grandmother when in person—even though you are quite familiar with and close to both of them—the same care should be taken when writing. The same goes for writing to people in business situations or to people you are unfamiliar with.

Tone of Voice

Your audience establishes your tone of voice. The tone of the letter should match the formality of the letter—more serious for business issues and letters to people you don't know well, more casual for family and friends. The only exception is with business associates who are also friends. If you are writing regarding business, keep the tone professional. If you are writing about social or personal issues, avoid sending such correspondence to their office. But if you must use their business contact information, still keep the tone professional. We often blur the lines of professionalism and friendship, but you should avoid this in your writing. Your tone of voice will also help establish the vocabulary that you choose, including forms of addressing the recipient of your letter.

Recipients

It is always best to find out as much as possible about addressing the intended recipient of your letter, whether you're writing to the principal of your child's school, a contractor, or a business. In some cases, that attention to detail may be important in getting past the screening process. If you cannot get a name or any additional information, never address a letter "Dear Sirs" or "Dear Gentlemen" unless you know with absolute certainty that the people reading it are all male. Of course, assuming that all the recipients are male today is an antiquated and gender-biased point of view. Instead, opt for "To Whom It May Concern," which is an acceptable, gender-free salutation.

CHOOSING YOUR WORDS

The body of a letter should have short, clear sentences written in the active voice. You are cringing, I know. Suddenly, the voice of your seventh-grade English teacher is screaming in the back of your head, and images of sentence diagrams on a chalkboard are floating in your mind. However, it's pretty simple. The active voice is a sentence where the subject is doing the action. For example, "The author wrote the book" is in the active voice. "The book was written by the author" uses the passive voice. Without the active voice, sentences get wordy and cumbersome. The active voice is direct and more concise than the passive voice. There are times when the passive voice is appropriate, such as recalling a story, but as a general rule, avoid using it.

Consider your audience and the intent of your letter when considering your choice of words and voice. Avoid long terms and phrases, archaic terms, and colloquial terms, especially in business and formal writing.

Length

Nobody wants to open an envelope and read a novel, which is another reason why you should use the active voice. Try to keep the overall length to one page, but no more than two. Use short, clear sentences and relatively short paragraphs. Be direct.

Not All Fonts Are Created Equal

If you are not handwriting your letter, its appearance relies on your font choice. There are hundreds of standard fonts, and graphic designers and other media artists develop new ones every day. While some fonts are decorative, if you are using a computer for writing, you should use a legible font. By legible, we mean the easiest to read with respect to size, weight, and spacing. The font helps create a snapshot of your letter and gives the reader all the visual clues they need when they read the letter.

If text looks too dense, the print too small, and the letters and line spacing too close together, are you really going to read it? Are you going to read all of it, or are you just going to quickly skim it? If you do intend to read it, will you read it right away, or will you set it aside to read later when you've got more time? You know the answer. Very few of us have time to read something that looks like it's going to be a chore to get through. This means that if you want your reader to actually read your writing and read it right away, you've got to give them a visual hook. And that visual hook is a clean, clear font that is well spaced and not too small. This is also the same reason for writing short, clear sentences and small paragraphs whenever possible.

When choosing a font, select a font with a serif and one where the letters are not spaced too close together. A serif font is one where the letters have "hats" and "feet" whereas sans serif fonts have neither. Good fonts to use are Times New Roman, Garamond, Book Antiqua, Palatino, and Georgia at any size between 10 point and 12 point. (The exception is when you're choosing a font for your letterhead, monogram, logo, or other text for which a stylized and creative font is acceptable and encouraged.)

Line Spacing and Margins

In letters, the spacing between lines within a paragraph should be single-spaced and spacing between paragraphs is double-spaced. With the exception of a page header, the distance from the top edge of a page to the first line of text should usually have margins no smaller than one inch in all directions. A page header, such as a business address or your name and other identifying information, should be no less than a half-inch from the top of the page, and all other margins set at one inch.

EDIT AND REWRITE

After you have written your draft, read it aloud. This may sound ridiculous, but reading it aloud, even to the dog, will help you hear how your writing sounds. Does the grammar make sense? Did you really convey what you meant, or is the tone going to deliver the wrong message? These are all things to consider when writing a letter, because unlike communication by telephone or in person, the reader does not have the benefit of hearing your voice or your inflection or seeing your body language, all of which are nonverbal signs and cues that we use to help determine someone's meaning. Grammatical and structural issues—for example, a misplaced or omitted comma—can create an entirely different meaning than the one you intend.

If you are reading aloud to someone other than your dog, such as someone who can actually offer good, critical, and constructive feedback, take it. (The only time this method may not be wise is when you're sending that love letter to your sweetie.) The great thing about having your spouse, roommate, trusted colleague, advisor, or anyone you like listen to the letter is that they can let you know if the letter makes sense to someone other than yourself. It is so easy to know what you are saying and feel that what you have written is obvious, but it is another thing to communicate what you want to say in a way that someone else can understand it. Those second pairs of eyes and ears will help you realize if something sounds too harsh, doesn't make sense, or has a strange flow, and avoid a host of other potential pitfalls. Your second pair of eyes and ears will also help you catch the things that spell-check will inevitably miss, such as those dreaded typos that are, in fact, real words. You know what I'm talking about. We've all done it.

PREPARING TO SEND YOUR LETTER

You have used the appropriate tools for your letter, set the margins and font accordingly, and crafted your prose to the appropriate audience. You've made at least one draft, finished the necessary edits, and are ready to send off the final piece of written work. Finally, it's time to prepare your document for mailing.

If you are using the postal system, make sure that your envelope is of the same weight and type as your paper. Be consistent with the font of your envelope as well. The post office does not like illegible fonts, and if the postal workers and carriers cannot read what you have written, the letter may not reach its destination. Before addressing your envelope, make sure that you have all of the correct postal information. You should have already done that when you prepared the inside address.

Most word-processing programs today provide you with the "labels" or "envelopes" function and will import the addressee's information for you to print the envelope or a label. Even so, it is still good to know the parts of the envelope and how to format them, especially if the computer or printer crashes, or you find yourself woefully out of ink at precisely the wrong time.

Labels Versus Printed Envelopes

For large batches of mail, such as to a group, the address label is acceptable, especially on larger envelopes. However, if your printer can print on envelopes, it is better to use this feature. Whether you handwrite or mechanically print your envelopes depends on your letter and should match the letter's style. With a few exceptions, business correspondence should always be mechanically printed.

Addressee Information

The addressee's information, also called the delivery address, is placed on the center of the front of the envelope and should be formatted as follows:

Ms. Beth Snyder, CEO
Suite 100
ABC Corporation
7600 Big Oil Avenue
Houston, TX 77506

Be sure to place the address high enough on the envelope to accommodate the bar code that the post office may print on the letter after it is received. Also, make sure that the address is not so high that it interferes with cancellation or franking of the postage. According to U.S. Postal Service guidelines in *A Customer's Guide to Mailing*, you should

* Print or type your return address in the upper left-hand corner on the front of the envelope.

* Use a stamp, postage meter, or PC postage to affix the correct amount.

* Clearly print the delivery address parallel to the longest side of the package or envelope.

* Not use commas or periods and find the correct spelling of a city, town, state, and the correct ZIP Code.

The post office also suggests that the address text is legible from an arm's length away.

Preparing the Envelope

Holding the envelope horizontally with the back flap facing downward, place your information in the upper left-hand corner. This area is called the corner card and should be formatted single-spaced as follows:

Mr. Alvin Gerber
1234 Main Street
St. Claire Shores, MI 48081

But if writing from a place of business, the format is like this:

Mr. Alvin Gerber
Suite 23
XYZ Corporation
5000 Main Street
St. Claire Shores, MI 48081

You will notice that Suite 23 appears before the name of the company. It intuitively seems incorrect, but the post office likes to see addresses in the location order of smallest to largest. The same rule goes for the addressee's information. Some people put their return address on the back flap of the envelope. This is acceptable to the post office—they will still deliver the letter—but consider your postal worker, who has to flip the envelope over to figure out the return address. And what if they had to do that with all the millions of pieces of mail that pass through their offices daily? You get the picture—just put the return address on the front of the envelope.

Special Addressing Circumstances

International addresses should be printed in all uppercase letters and should conform to the following specifications set forth by the United States Postal Service:

If possible, addresses should have no more than five lines. The full address should be typed or legibly written in English, using Roman letters and Arabic numerals, and should be placed lengthwise on one side of the item. An address in a foreign language is permitted if the names of the city, province, and country are also indicated in English.

The last line of the address block area must include only the complete country name (no abbreviations) written in uppercase letters.

Foreign postal codes, if used, should be placed on the line above the destination country. Some countries prefer that the postal code follow the name, while others prefer that it precede the city or town name. The following shows the order of information for the destination address, which should be single-spaced:

Line 1: NAME OF ADDRESSEE

Line 2: STREET ADDRESS/POST OFFICE BOX NUMBER

Line 3: CITY OR TOWN NAME, OTHER PRINCIPLE SUBDIVISION (such as PROVINCE, STATE, or COUNTY) AND POSTAL CODE (if known).

Note: In some countries, the postal code may precede the city or town name, so follow the postal conventions where the letter or package is being mailed.

Line 4: COUNTRY NAME (in uppercase letters and in English)

The following are examples given by the Post Office of properly formatted delivery addresses for an international letter:

MS JOYCE BROWNING
2045 ROYAL ROAD
LONDON WIP 6HQ
ENGLAND

MS JOYCE BROWNING
2045 ROYAL ROAD
06570 ST PAUL
FRANCE

The following format should be used for addresses to Canada:

MS HELEN SAUNDERS
1010 CLEAR STREET
OTTAWA ON K1A 0B1
CANADA

Notice that for Canadian addresses, the province abbreviation is placed between the city and the postal code. Also, pay attention when describing postal codes; they are only called "ZIP Codes" in the United States. ZIP is the acronym for Zone Improvement Plan, and its use was started in the 1960s in order for the postal service to better handle increased volumes of mail.

The sender's address (return address or corner card) should also be in all uppercase letters, and the country written on the line below the city, state, and ZIP Code. So, if Mr. Gerber from our previous example is sending a letter overseas, his address should look like this:

MR. ALVIN GERBER
1234 MAIN STREET
ST. CLAIRE SHORES, MI 48081
USA

Alternatively, you can write out UNITED STATES or UNITED STATES OF AMERICA instead of USA.

Postage

Make sure that your letter has the correct postage for domestic or international mailing. Postage rates depend on the weight and size of the letter including any enclosures. Postage is affixed or printed on the upper right-hand corner of the envelope and should not have anything over it, such as tape. You can determine the correct postage by taking the letter to the post office, or if you have a postal scale available to you, using it to calculate the correct postage. For mailed items that require inserts and return cards, such as wedding invitations, you should consider the weight of the entire package including external and internal stamps before purchasing your stamps and mailing your documents.

Filling the Envelope

This section may seem like a no-brainer, but it is important because the presentation of the opened envelope is just as important as the meat of your letter. For a simple letter that is no more than two pages and contains no enclosures, fold the letter in thirds and insert it into the envelope so that the top flap is facing down. This way, the recipient will immediately see from and to whom the letter is and the first line of the letter when he or she opens it. For simple letters with enclosures that require a larger envelope, place the enclosures behind the cover letter in the order in which they are to be viewed and place them in the envelope so that the text faces the back of the envelope. This way, the recipient can immediately see from and to whom it is sent without having to turn the letter over.

Cards

Cards should be placed in the envelope with the fold facing down and the front of the card facing the rear of the envelope. This is so the card is not accidentally cut if the recipient uses a letter opener with a sharp edge. It also ensures that if there are any enclosures in the envelope, such as short notes, photographs, or money, they stay near the fold of the card and also have less of a chance of becoming victim to the sharp letter opener.

Now, off you go to mail your beautifully arranged packages and well-written letters!

✳ Chapter 2 ✳
Saying Thank You

The thank-you note is a simple yet complex piece of writing. They are simple because they are easy to find—from neat little boxed packages that you can purchase almost anywhere in a variety of styles for nearly any occasion to singular cards. They are complex because they are deeply personal—both for the sender and the receiver.

THE THANK-YOU NOTE TODAY

Most people were raised with the notion that sending a thank-you note is the correct and polite thing to do. It is a mistake to assume the thank-you note is an antiquated notion. The thank-you note serves three purposes. First, it acknowledges receipt of and/or appreciation for what has been done. Second, it tells the giver something about you and your character. Thirdly, it shows the recipient that you think well of them enough to take a few moments to write them a quick note. What a way to brighten someone's day!

The realm of thank-you notes covers those for gifts and other niceties bestowed upon us as well as in the business realm where one expresses gratitude for another's time or actions. The contents of a thank-you note should never be generic and should be written in a way that addresses the individual you are thanking and what you are thanking them for. While you don't want to write one on a cocktail napkin, a thank-you note does not need to be fancy or on ornate thank-you stationery.

WRITING THE THANK-YOU NOTE

Think about what you want to say and use the active voice. Format the note with your name and address, followed by the date, and the recipient's name and address, using semi-block format. For business-related thank-you notes, block format is also acceptable. Business-related thank you notes should be typed. Personal thank-you notes can be handwritten or typed. Thank-you notes should always be signed.

The General Thank-You Note

The general thank-you note is for gifts, parties, and other social events. It is usually a folded note card on good card stock. The outside usually says, "Thank You" or "Thanks," alerting the recipient of the contents. The inside is where you craft your simple, handwritten prose. Here is a sweet and simple example:

Dear Aunt Susan,

Thank you for the slow-cooker and Grandma's stew recipes as a housewarming gift. You remembered how much I loved her stews growing up, and knowing how much work she put into them, you've given me an easy way to make them! When you come into town next, we'll have to sit down and chat over some warm bowls of stew. Hopefully, I can do justice to Grandma's recipes!

With much love and appreciation,

Lizzy

Note that Lizzy's signature should be an actual signature. This thank-you note doesn't just tell Aunt Susan "thanks," but expresses something personal about the gift and why it is appreciated.

Whether or not Lizzy ends up using the slow-cooker except for when Aunt Susan comes into town is irrelevant—the note will make Susan feel as though her gift is truly appreciated. It also reminds Susan what the gift was for. This is important. It doesn't suggest that Susan is feeble and can't remember why she sent the gift, but let's face it, in the course of a given year, we may receive (or send) many gifts to a single person for birthdays, anniversaries, Christmas and Hanukkah, housewarming parties, wedding and baby showers, and the list goes on. So indicating which gift and for what is a good idea, especially if the thank-you note does not follow immediately upon receipt of the gift.

Timing of a Thank-You Note

The window for sending a thank-you note varies from situation to situation, and the opinions about when a thank-you note should be sent varies as well. Ideally, thank-you notes should be sent out as soon as possible after a gift has been received. The clear exceptions for this are thank-you notes for wedding gifts, where the new bride and groom customarily have up to three months from the wedding date to respond to gifts received at or after the wedding. The reasons for such a long lead time between receiving the gifts and sending the thank-you notes in this situation is purely about the realities of time. Since the newly married couple usually goes on some sort of honeymoon after the ceremony, they return home to gifts that may have been opened prior to their leaving as well as any gifts that may have arrived during their absence—gift-givers have a year to send gifts to the new couple.

Faced with the duties of setting up their home together and establishing their new life, anyone who has been through this ritual of life knows that sitting down to write 200 thank-you notes at once would require another vacation in itself. So brides and grooms are given a bit of a break when it comes to wedding gifts. Gifts for bridal showers and bachelor parties are a different story, however. Thank-you notes should be sent within a week of the bridal shower or bachelor party. They should not only be sent to guests who brought gifts but also to the hosts of the parties.

Unfortunately, new mothers do not get the same break as newly married couples. Thank-you notes for baby showers should also be sent within a week of the shower. For gifts received after the baby is born, even as the new mother is faced with learning a whole slew of new information, some advocate writing the thank-you note immediately upon receipt of a gift. We all know that doing so is not always possible, so a good rule of thumb to follow is to get the thank-you note out within a week of having received a gift.

THANKING A GROUP

Sometimes gifts are given from a group of people. The proper way to thank the group is to send a personal thank-you note to each person from the group. However, this is not always possible because you might not know which people in the group participated, such as when an organization has gathered together to give a gift or donate money to a cause. Therefore, it's a good idea to simply send the note to the group president or leader.

Dear Jennifer,

I received the gift from the ladies of the Auxiliary Club that you sent with my husband after the last Council meeting. I was so surprised when he came home with that adorable package! Thank you so much for the receiving blankets, onesies, bath toys and towels, teddy bear, and outfits. We were so touched! Please also extend my sincerest thanks and appreciation to everyone for thinking of us. I'm looking forward to attending meetings again after the baby is born.

Fondly,

Debbie

Jennifer understood that the thank you was intended for those women who actually participated and read the note aloud at the next meeting. Debbie fulfilled her mom-to-be thank-you-note duties without embarrassing the people who did not participate in the gift giving.

THANK-YOU NOTES FROM BABIES AND VERY YOUNG CHILDREN

Though you may be tempted to write thank-you notes in the voice of your baby or young child, it should not be done.

It is ridiculous that your baby or young child—who is neither reading nor writing yet—has crafted thank-you-note prose. Instead, a parent should write the note in his or her own voice, expressing thanks for the gift on behalf of the child.

If you absolutely cannot override the cute impulse to pen the thank-you notes in the child's voice, save those for your closest family members, such as Grandma or a dear uncle, who are probably the only people receiving the thank-you notes who will share your sense of cuteness. If the child is old enough, however, he or she can sign their name or draw a little picture as a signature. For children who are verbal but cannot write well yet, they can dictate their thanks as parents write the note, and the child can still "sign" the thank-you note.

Thank-You Note from a Child

Dear Mike and Kathy,

Thank you for coming to Matthew's first birthday party. Dan and I were so glad to see you, and we really appreciate the great train set! Matthew is quite fascinated by the engine and loves saying "choo, choo" when he plays with it. I secretly think that Dan loves playing with it as much as Matthew does. Looking forward to seeing everyone at Thanksgiving!

Love always,

Marcia

THANK-YOU NOTES FOR HOSPITALITY

Hospitality is an occasion in which people often forget to send a thank-you note. Not all situations require a thank-you note, but a good rule of thumb is that it is polite and wise to send a thank-you note for hospitality the longer the stay was or the more involved the gathering was. Examples of when to send a hospitality-related thank-you note include when you stay overnight or longer at a friend's house, if someone takes care of your hotel accommodations for an event, or when you were invited to an elaborate gathering. While some may believe that the quick phone call or e-mail suffices for these situations, a thank-you note will be appreciated greatly by the recipient.

Thank-You Note from Overnight Guests

Dear Marcia,

We had such a lovely weekend at the beach house, and we appreciate you and Dan hosting us. Caitlin had a blast playing "big sister" to Matthew as she calls it. Everything now is about "Baby Matthew." And there was nothing quite like watching our husbands transform into the summertime superheroes Grill Man and Burger Meister. Looking forward to having you stay with us when you come into town next month for the festival!

Much love,

Kathy

Thank-You Note from a Party Guest

Dear Brian and Liz,

As always, you threw a fabulous New Year's Eve party! I think you may have outdone yourselves this year. Thanks for inviting Michael and me to what proved to be yet another memorable evening! Best wishes for a happy new year.

Yours,

Sarah

You might have noticed something in the above examples. The letters are all from an individual even though it is implied that the thanks expressed are from the couple. This is perfectly acceptable, as only the actual writer of the thank-you note needs to sign it.

THANK-YOU-NOTE CUSTOMS

A recent trend during social gatherings, such as showers, is to have each of the guests fill out their address on an envelope that the bride or mother-to-be supplies. This seems like a good idea on the surface, as it gives the guest of honor one less thing to do when she writes her notes. But really, what it does is puts the guests on the spot. What if one of them has yet to supply a gift? Furthermore, the guest of honor probably already has everyone's addresses, as in the case of a wedding, when it is highly likely that the guests at her shower are also invited to the wedding. In events such as a baby shower where the guests are probably not going to be part of the culminating happy event, the hostess or hostesses can give the guest of honor everyone's address separately.

One very good idea during such an event—or other party where large quantities of gifts will be opened—is to have someone keep a gift log. As gifts are opened and cards are read, someone records who gave what gift. This way the honoree can aptly address his or her thank-you notes to the correct person for the correct gift.

THANK-YOU NOTES FOR MONETARY GIFTS

Notes about monetary gifts can be somewhat touchy. This is the instance where you can be a bit vaguer in the body of the note because some people do not like to discuss money in any capacity. Presumably, the person you are thanking is aware of how much they gave you. But you should still express the same kind of gratitude and sincerity for the monetary gift as you would any other gift.

Thank-You Note for a Monetary Gift

Dear Uncle Jonathan,

I am sorry that you couldn't join us for my graduation party, and I missed you terribly. Thank you for the monetary gift that you sent. I really appreciate it, and it will definitely come in handy when I start college in the fall. I hope to see you soon!

Your favorite nephew,

Nicholas

THANK-YOU NOTES IN BUSINESS

The business thank-you note is different from the social thank-you note. It should be printed on company letterhead or personal business stationery and should follow a similar format to the social thank-you note. However, there should be a higher degree of formality in the tone.

The Post-Job Interview Thank-You Note

Many business professionals will tell you that few job candidates send thank-you notes to their recruiters, headhunters, or interviewers. This fact is appalling, and given the low proportion of thank-you notes written, the professional graciousness and courtesy that you show by sending a thank-you note will set you apart from countless other candidates for the position.

In many industries, sending your thank-you note by e-mail has become standard practice, and it has the advantage of promptness, as you do not know when hiring decisions will be made. As with any professional e-mail, make sure that the subject line is clear. In either mailed or e-mailed format, as with all formal business letters, you should formally address the recipient with Mr., Mrs., or Ms. In the body of the letter, thank the person with whom you met for their time and highlight key points from the interview. The letter should be no longer than one page.

Business Thank-You Note

John Smith
123 Main Street
New York, NY 10013

September 5, 2014

Ms. Melissa Bear, CEO
Bear and Company
789 West 57th Street
New York, NY 10001

Dear Ms. Bear:

It was a pleasure meeting with you today. Thank you for taking the time out of your schedule to discuss the Account Executive position and introducing me to the other members of your staff. I am inspired by the innovative approaches to customer service and customer retention that have made Bear and Company a leader in the field. I am confident that my experience, skill set, and ability to learn quickly in a fast-paced environment will make me an asset to the team.

I look forward to hearing from you about the position. If you have further questions for me or need additional information, I can be reached at 212-555-1234 or via e-mail at jsmith@myisp.com.

Sincerely yours,

John Smith

John Smith

John's thank-you note to Ms. Bear informs her not only of his gratitude, but makes specific reference to his interview. Surely Ms. Bear is interviewing other candidates for the position, so his note serves to remind her who he was and why she wanted to interview him in the first place. It also shows Ms. Bear that John knows how to write a business letter, and that this kind of mutual respect is one that he would probably afford other people with whom he would have contact if he were to get the position.

THE COLLEAGUE-TO-COLLEAGUE THANK-YOU NOTE

When thanking colleagues, administrators, or subordinates, the business thank-you note can be a little less formal, but it should still sound professional, regardless of whether it is sent by the U.S. Post Office, interoffice mail, or e-mail. Our examples below involve mailed letters, but the format would be much the same for e-mail as well.

Unless the gratitude is for something outside the realm of business, the note should be on company letterhead and addressed to the person's business address. If several people were involved, you can opt to send a singular, general letter depending on how many people were instrumental. If only a few people were involved, a separate thank-you note should be written to each person with a brief detail about what you are thanking them for. Whenever possible, send a carbon copy (cc) of the same note to the individual's immediate supervisor so that the commendation can be included in their employee file.

To an Individual

Company Letterhead

(Note, when using the company letterhead, there is no need to include the company address again).

September 10, 2014

Avril Johnson
Assistant Manager
Research Department

Dear Avril,

Thank you for examining the client records that I provided regarding Mr. Smith's account. I appreciate how quickly you returned the information to me so that we could resolve his questions. I look forward to working with you again in the future.

Sincerely yours,

Michael Hooper

Michael Hooper
Account Executive
Client Services

cc: Beth Johnson, Research Department Supervisor

To a Group

Company Letterhead

September 15, 2014

Dear Fundraising Events Team:

Thank you for all of your efforts in putting on a spectacular fundraiser! The Shooting for the Stars evening on September 9th was a success. The event generated $100,000, 10 percent over our goal. Special thanks go out to Andrea Anderson, who coordinated the evening, and Charles Steinberg, her co-chair for planning the event. We are looking forward to next year's event, which I am sure will be just as much of a success.

Sincerely,

Fred McCloud

Fred McCloud
Department of Leadership and Development

cc: Andrea Anderson
    William Colby
    Rachel Emerson
    Susan Murphy
    Fred Murray
    Nick Smith
    Bethany Smithson
    Charles Steinberg

THANK-YOU NOTES FOR RECEIVING A GIFT OR CONTRIBUTION

Thank-you notes in recognition of a gift or contribution for a business entity should be short and to the point. In this case, the thank-you note serves two purposes. First, it acknowledges receipt and gratitude. Second, if applicable, it can serve as a receipt for the donor. As with any business correspondence, the thank-you note should be printed on company letterhead.

Thank-You Note for a Gift or Contribution

Company Letterhead

September 24, 2014

Dear Mrs. Contributor:

Thank you for your generous contribution of $1,500 to the Shooting for the Stars fundraiser. We are sorry that you were unable to attend the event, but we appreciate your continued support of our development endeavors. We hope that we will see you at next year's event, and as always, we wish you the best.

Sincerely yours,

Ross Couch

Ross Couch
Senior Development Officer
Department of Leadership and Development

OOPS! REMEDYING THE FORGOTTEN THANK-YOU NOTE

In today's world, we are all very busy. Sometimes in our fast-paced and often hectic lives, we slip and forget to write a thank-you note. Or we manage to write one but forget to mail it. Don't fret, you can still send it. A late thank-you note is better than none at all. In your belated note, be honest without sounding as if you are making excuses. Indicate to the recipient how much you appreciated the act of kindness, and include a sincere apology for not getting the thank-you note out sooner.

Belated Thank-You Note

Dear Uncle Jeff,

We are so sorry for getting this thank-you note for the lovely doll that you sent Becca for her birthday out to you so late. I came down with the flu after nursing the kids back to health, and in trying to catch up with work and the household, I completely forgot to mail our thank-you note to you.

Becca loves the Suzi doll that you sent her! I have enclosed a picture of the two of them together for you, as well as a couple of shots from the party. We wish that you could have made it for the party and seen how wide her eyes opened when she looked in the box. We hope that you are doing well and look forward to seeing you soon.

Love,

Beth

Beth's letter was sincere and candid. Hopefully, Uncle Jeff will understand the situation, but at the very least, he won't think that Beth—on behalf of her daughter, Becca—is ungrateful.

USEFUL WORDS AND PHRASES

Thank you for your time.

✳

Thank you so much!

✳

Thank you for your generosity.

✳

Thanks for your hospitality.

✳

Grateful

✳

I/We appreciate…

✳

I/We enjoyed…

✳

Your … means so much to me/us.

✳

Thank you for your consideration.

*

With much love and appreciation

*

May life bring you a reflection of the
kindness you've shown to others.

*

Your kindness is appreciated.

*

A million thanks.

*

I'm overwhelmed by your generosity.

*

Thank you for your thoughtfulness.

*

Your kindness touched my heart.

*

I am forever thankful.

*

Your thoughtful gift brought a
smile to my face.

You always brighten my day.

✳

I'll always remember your kindness.

✳

May you be blessed for the kindness
you've shown me.

✳

Thank you for such a lovely time/evening.

✳

It was a pleasure...

✳

I/We am/are glad...

✳

Sincerely

✳

I am humbled by...

✳

Friends like you are a rare treasure.
Thank you for all that you've done.

✳

Thanks for all you've done for me.

Next time, it's my turn.

✳

Just saying thank you because you've
been thoughtful so often!

✳

My "thank you" seems so small compared to all
you've done, but it comes from my heart.

✳

Your kind gesture will last a lifetime.

✳

One person. One deed. A million thanks.

✳

You are a gift to my life. Thanks for everything.

✳

Knowing you're there to cheer me on is making
things so much easier. Thank you!

✳

For one person, you do an awful lot of good.

✳

It's a comfort to know we can count on each
other through whatever life brings.

✳

I am so lucky to have a friend like you.

✳

You always brighten my day. I'm so grateful.

✳

Your giving nature and unselfish ways are
a blessing to everyone who knows you.

✳

Some people give hugs. Some people give help.
You give your all.

✳

The way you come to the aid of others is wonderful.

✳

You are a treasure.

✳

Generosity is a sign of a great soul.
You've surely one.

✳

Sometimes simple words say it best. Thank you
from the bottom of my heart.

✳

Thank you—for what you did, what
you said, and who you are.

✳

You have a "gift for giving"!

*

May your thoughtfulness find its way back to you.

*

You've restored my faith. I'll be forever grateful.

*

A person like you brightens the world for the rest of us.

*

I will always be grateful to you for your
thoughtfulness and consideration.

TIPS

Do

* keep it simple.

* be sincere and gracious.

* use the active voice.

* send thank-you notes as soon as possible, if not within
  a week of receiving a gift.

* be specific about what you are writing to thank the
  person for.

* be sure that grammar is correct.

* sign your thank-you notes using a pen with quality ink.

* double-check the spelling of names and titles with a reliable source, such as a secretary or administrative assistant, for business-related thank-you notes.

* handwrite personal thank-you notes.

* use appropriate business stationery or letterhead.

* use the semi-block format for personal thank-you notes; block or memo format for business-related thank-you notes.

* find something gracious to say, even if you aren't entirely thrilled about the gift or experience.

Don't

* use a ballpoint pen, felt-tip pen, or permanent marker, because they can skip, smudge, or bleed through the note.

* write thank-you notes for children in the child's voice (unless the child is dictating their letter to you).

* sign another person's name. Only the writer needs to sign the note, even when writing on behalf of another party. (The only exception is in business, where a secretary or administrative assistant may be the actual writer.)

* let your thank-you note or letter be longer than one page.

* send personal thank-you notes to a person's business address.

* go on and on about why a late thank-you note is late. Be honest and brief.

⇒ Chapter 3 ⇐

Invitations

Invitations are one of the more common types of correspondence you'll write or receive. Dinner parties, birthday parties, graduation parties, and wedding and baby showers are just a few occasions that call for invitations.

Invitations officially alert people of an event. They should include information about the event, including its day and date, time, location, a reply date, and some kind of method for the recipient to reply.

Invitations can be either formal or casual, depending on the event you're hosting. The type of invitation should, therefore, match the formality and type of event. Invitations should be sent so that the invited have enough time to reply and make plans to attend, and the hosts or event planners can fully plan for the number of anticipated guests. With the exception of the impromptu gathering, invitation lead time is crucial, especially if you expect to have any guests attend your function. This includes your closest friends and family members who may already know about the event that you have been excitedly talking about for weeks. Remember, people are busy with obligations of their own, so don't assume that it's actually on their calendars just because you've been casually chatting about it for a month.

Though some view sending invitations as a pain, they also help you out—assuming that the recipients of the invitation take the time and care to reply in a timely fashion. For your own part, if you happen to receive an invitation, even if it's from someone as close to you as your next-door neighbor, best friend, or sister-in-law, you should take the time to reply in the manner requested in the invitation. If you replied stating that you would attend, but some other more pressing matter will prevent you from attending, make sure to inform the host as soon as you know of the change. If you're not yet sure if you'll be able to attend the event because of another engagement, do not officially accept. It's a good idea to contact the host as soon as possible and let them know you're unsure about being able to attend, but that you'll let them know as soon as you have more information.

For the most part, invitations should be simple. The basic anatomy of an invitation is:

Host's Name

Event

Day and Date

Location

Time

*Reply date and method with
the contact information*

The specific information that is in an invitation and its overall style informs the recipient of the type of event and the degree of formality. The type and style of the invitation also indicate the type of attire to wear. As a general rule, your attire should be more formal according to how fancy and formal the invitation is and how late in the day the event is scheduled, unless the host specifies otherwise in the invitation itself. For example, a wedding will be held at 7:30 P.M. in the evening, but the invitation specifically states "costume party," "come as you are," "business casual," or "white tie," to name a few examples. Before standard dress became more relaxed, "formal" meant "white tie" and "informal" meant "black tie." In contemporary modes of dress, "formal" usually means "black tie." Men, that means you're expected to break out the tuxedo, and women, that means a long dress or ball gown.

You can either start with preformatted invitations or you can create your own template in a publishing or word-processing program. If you are using a preformatted invitation, such as a boxed set of themed invitations or your personal invitation cards, legibly write the information by hand. It is better to write in cursive or script, but you can also write in print if your cursive looks like the directions on a physician's prescription pad. Whichever you choose, be sure that the information presented is legible, clear, and that the invitation is clean. For the more formal invitations, which might be printed or engraved by a professional printer, supply the text to the printing or engraving company. The formality of the event will determine the style and font of the printed or engraved invitation, unless you specifically choose a design or template from the printer's or engraver's style catalog.

HOW TO WRITE IT

Before you start writing your invitation, think about the event, the time, how formal the event is (black tie or casual, for example), and whether the event has a theme. Then, look at the calendar and allow enough time to address issues of food, drink, and decorations. If you are using a caterer, they will help determine when you will need a final head count. Use that date to guide your reply date. A good general rule of thumb is to make the reply date at least one week prior to the date of the event. Count back from your reply date (four to six weeks for informal events and six to eight weeks for formal events) to determine the target date by which your invited guests should receive the invitation.

In your invitation, include who is hosting the party, the day and date of the event, the time the party starts—or if it is during a set time, the exact time frame for the event—information about the location including the address, and a way for invited guests to reply to the invitation. Directions to the location should also be included as an insert or on a separate card or sheet of paper if it is for a formal event. Include information about nearby accommodations when sending invitations to out-of-town guests (unless the guests are staying in your home). If there are special instructions, such as "wear something comfortable," include that information on the invitation as well.

Note that when sending invitations to unmarried people, etiquette dictates that only the people named on the invitation are actually invited. If the unmarried people are engaged or are in an otherwise long-term relationship, both names should be included on the invitation.

INVITATION EXAMPLES

The following examples are arranged from least formal to most formal.

A Casual Party

Please Join BETH and LARRY for their Annual Summer Beach Party!

Saturday, August 16, 2014

3:30 P.M.

3225 Beech Tree Lane

West Egg, New York

This year's theme is a Tiki Party!

Hawaiian attire is encouraged.

R.S.V.P. by August 1, 2014, by calling us at 516-555-9999 or by e-mailing Beth at BethWilliams@myisp.com

Beth and Larry have sent this invitation to 50 guests. Ideally, the invitation has been sent out four to six weeks prior to the event, meaning that the recipients *receive* the invitation four to six weeks before the event. Chances are that the invited guests are local. If the invited guests have attended Beth and Larry's annual summer beach party in previous years, they probably anticipate its occurrence and already have it on their calendar. But the invitation serves as a reminder and gives Beth and Larry enough time to plan adequately for the number of anticipated guests.

Because the event starts in the afternoon and is a beach party, the recipient can assume that the attire is beach casual, but Larry and Beth have also given their possible guests another clue by informing them that the theme is a Tiki Party and that, while not mandatory, Hawaiian attire is welcome at the event. This type of event can either be designed as a traditional fold-over card, a single, flat card, or as a flyer—that is, on a full 8 1/2 by 11-inch sheet.

You may have noticed that the response line does not say "Please R.S.V.P." That is because to add "please" to the line would be redundant. R.S.V.P. is an abbreviation for the French phrase *Répondez s'il vous plaît*. To translate the phrase into English, it means "Respond, if you please." Additionally, "if you please" does not mean that a response is optional. It is just a polite way of informing the invited guest that a reply is expected.

One can also opt to write "Please reply by" as an alternative to R.S.V.P. Another variant on the "Please reply" line is "Regrets only," meaning the recipient of the invitation is to only respond if they cannot attend.

Business Casual Event

Some events are a bit more formal, and the purpose of the event is beyond a simple party. These events are often business casual or semi-formal and may be business-related. Business casual implies an event where formal wear is not required, but jeans or shorts will be entirely inappropriate and formal wear would be over the top.

> **The Foundation for Really Cool Stuff**
> **announces its third annual**
> **Founder's Day Dinner and Holiday Party**
>
> **Please join us at**
> **the Westin Hotel in the Sherman Ballroom**
> **1 Huntington Avenue**
> **Boston, Massachusetts, 02116**
> **Friday, December 13, 2013**
> **6:30 P.M. to 11:30 P.M.**
> **for dinner, dancing, and awards**
>
> **Please reply by November 30, 2013,**
> **by calling Julia MacMurtrie at**
> **617-555-1234**

The location—a four-star hotel—and time of day indicates that the event is business casual or semi-formal. Indicating the overall plan for the evening also informs the recipient what to expect. As with Beth and Larry's annual summer beach party, this invitation will have been sent out so that the recipients receive it by November 2, 2013, if not earlier, especially to account for the Thanksgiving holiday and giving people enough time to reply.

FORMAL EVENTS

Invitations to formal events such as weddings or black-tie dinners should be engraved or professionally printed on card stock or a good bond paper. Unlike the less formal invitations, these invitations include a reply card that the recipient will return to the host of the event. While the overall language of a formal invitation is the same as for other invitations, the phrasing of the opening line will vary depending on who the hosts are.

Wedding Invitation

Mr. and Mrs. Jonathan Blake
and
Mr. and Dr. Anthony Edwards
Request the honor of your presence at the
Marriage of
Miss Elizabeth Ann Blake and Mr. Michael Edwards
on
Saturday, May 17, 2014
At 3:30 in the afternoon
at
the estate of Mrs. Wilma Andrews
60972 Oxbow Road
Chicago, Illinois

Reception to follow

R.S.V.P. by April 2, 2014

In a formal invitation, all words excluding numerals and titles are written out. It should also be noted that as an alternative to the convention of writing "Mr. and Mrs." or "Mr. and Dr.," the first and last names of the parents could be written out either with or without their respective titles.

Jonathan and Felicia Blake

and

Anthony and Sarah Edwards

or

Mr. Jonathan and Mrs. Felicia Blake

and

Mr. Anthony and Dr. Sarah Edwards

If the bride and groom are of ages where they are inviting the guests themselves, then the invitation is from them and not the respective parents of the couple. The rule of thumb for such formal invitations is that whoever is paying for the event gets to have their names on the invitations as the hosts.

Formal Wedding Invitation by the Bride and Groom

MISS AMANDA ELYSE SCHOENINGER

AND

MR. MATTHEW JASON BROCKENSTOCK

REQUEST THE HONOR OF YOUR PRESENCE

AT THEIR WEDDING

ON

SATURDAY, MAY 17, 2014

AT

2:30 IN THE AFTERNOON

AT

TEMPLE BETH EL

3200 GRAND BOULEVARD

BLOOMFIELD HILLS, MICHIGAN

KIDDUSH AND RECEPTION TO FOLLOW

Formal Golden Anniversary Party

Susan and Jonathan Edwards,
Matthew Payne
and
Sarah Payne
Request the honor of your presence at the celebration of
the Golden Anniversary of their parents,
Andrew and Miriam Payne,
on Saturday, June 14, 2014,
at seven o'clock in the evening
at the Woodlands Country Club
59032 Country Club Lane
Gibraltar, Michigan

Please reply by May 3, 2014

In this case, you can see that the children of the guests of honor are throwing their parents a golden anniversary party, and that the hosts of the party are listed in order of chronological age. Clearly, Susan is the eldest child and is already married, and thus uses her married name. Since her husband and parents are on excellent terms, he is also included as one of the hosts, even though he is not the biological child of the guests of honor. Alternatively, the invitation could have read "Susan Payne Edwards" even if Susan does not usually use her maiden name. Because Susan is the first person listed, even if all three children are "hosting" the party, the reply cards should be addressed to Susan and Jonathan Edwards. Additionally, even though the husband's name usually precedes the wife's, in this case Susan's name precedes his because Jonathan is not the biological child of Mr. and Mrs. Payne. Sorry, Jonathan and other dear husbands, but when he and his siblings host a party for his parents, his name will precede his wife's.

You will note that the Payne children did not indicate the type of dress or formality of the event. The invited guests, who are probably a mixture of family, friends, and their parents' peers, will know based on the type of invitation, the location, and the time of evening that the event is contemporary formal or black-tie.

THE REPLY CARD

The reply card for a formal event is a smaller card that, like the invitation, is engraved or professionally printed. The reply-card envelope should, at the very least, include the address of the hosts in the addressee section. It is a nice touch and easier on your invited guests to also include the appropriate postage on the reply card. Also be sure that the reply cards conform to postal regulations. Other methods to reply include the letter of acceptance or letter of regret, which are discussed later.

Reply card example:

Please reply by May 3, 2014

M._____

___ *Accepts with pleasure*

___ *Declines with regrets*

The invitation and the reply card are placed in a foil-lined envelope, often with liner paper between the invitation and the reply card. Other formal or otherwise solemn events follow this same convention.

RITES OF PASSAGE

Aside from weddings, a rite of passage already discussed, there are other significant periods in one's life that warrant celebrating. As we go through life, the transition from childhood to adulthood is a special time marked by religious, secular, or cultural ceremonies. Sometimes these ceremonies overlap, occurring within a short number of years. Bar and Bat Mitzvahs, confirmations, cotillions, *quinceañeras*, and sweet sixteen parties are just a few. Other rites of passage can occur earlier or later in a person's life, such as First Communion or graduation.

Bar and Bat Mitzvahs, Confirmations, and Other Religious Rites of Passage

Because these religious ceremonies are co-hosted by parents and the related religious institution, there are two parts to these events—first, the actual ceremony, where guests will bear witness to the spiritual and cultural transition of the candidate; and second, a small reception or party in honor of the young person who has entered a new stage in their spiritual journey. As with other events, the formality of the invitation matches that of the corresponding party. While these milestones are important, it is important to remember that the main event celebrated is the religious rite of passage and not the bash afterward.

Example of Bar/Bat Mitzvah:

Mr. and Mrs. Jacob Steinman

Request the honor of your presence as

Alexis Steinman

is called to the Torah as a Bat Mitzvah (choose correct gender)

on

Saturday, May 17, 2014,

at

Ten-thirty in the morning

at

Congregation Beth El

151 Maple Leaf Lane

Rochester, New York

Kiddush to Follow

A secondary invitation may also be included to a party that is held after the main event. The beauty of using a second invitation is that you can be selective in who is invited to the non-religious part of the event, if you so choose. For example, if the parents' closest friends and colleagues are also invited to the religious ceremony, but the parents prefer to only invite the Rabbi and his wife, close family members, the inner-most circle of family friends, and a few of their child's closest friends to their home, it gives them the opportunity to do so tastefully.

Secondary Invitation:

> *Please join us for a small party in honor of*
> *Alexis's Bat Mitzvah*
>
> *From 4:00 to 7:00 P.M.,*
> *at our home,*
> *5677 Baldpate Hill Road*
> *Hilton Head, South Carolina*
>
> *Regrets only 724-555-0981*

Both parts of the invitation should be included in the same exterior envelope. The invitation to the ceremony does not need a specific reply card, unless there are space limitations at the building.

In the event of confirmations or first communions, where several candidates may be accepting the rite at the same time, the church may provide invitations or a template for invitations. These ceremonies are usually held in conjunction with usual Sunday services or Mass, and an announcement of the ceremonies and the names of the candidates may be published in the church bulletin or newsletter. If the church does not provide invitations beyond what is printed in the bulletin or newsletter, parents can send out their own to notify the people they would like to attend the ceremony but are not members of their church. Because both of these ceremonies are one of several Christian initiation rites that a person may take over the course of a lifetime (for example, both are one of the seven sacraments for Catholics), it is best to keep the invitations simple, such as on a flat card. An additional reply card is optional, but you also want to include reply information on the invitation.

Confirmation or First Communion:

Please join us in bearing witness as
Chandler Francis Ablemarle
makes his
First Communion
on
Sunday, June 21, 2014,
at
Eleven in the morning
at
St. John the Evangelist Church
2300 Westlake Street
Minneapolis, Minnesota

Light reception honoring the new First Communicants
to follow immediately after the ceremony
in the church hall.

Luncheon to follow the small reception
at The Big Bear Lodge
5700 Westlake Street
Minneapolis, Minnesota

Please reply by June 8, 2014
218-555-9876

Cotillions, *Quinceañeras*, Sweet Sixteen Parties, and Other Secular and Social Rites of Passage

Most people will experience both religious and secular or social rites of passage. Social and secular rites of passage include graduations from high school, college, and other institutions of higher education, cotillions or debutante balls, sweet sixteen parties, *quinceañeras*—a Latino/a tradition—and prom. These events represent the presentation of a completion of a stage, whether in one's education or professional life or marking a new chronological age that may also come with new responsibilities. In some ways, the cotillion and *quinceañera* are secular equivalents of the Bar/Bat Mitzvah or Confirmation, which represent a transition from childhood into adult society.

Invitations to graduations and proms are often provided by the school through the graduation committee, Dean's office, or prom committee. Oftentimes graduates are given a set number of invitations, sometimes issued with tickets depending on the size of the school, and they needn't do anything further. If the parents of the graduates or the graduates themselves plan to host an event after the ceremonies, they should send out separate invitations. The separate invitation should only be for the party and not include the graduation, since capacity for the graduation ceremonies is predetermined. Don't worry about offending people who want to attend the graduation ceremony—they will understand the space limitations and will be honored that you wish to celebrate with them, even if they don't get to physically see the graduate receive his or her diploma.

Cotillions, *quinceañera*, proms, and other social rites of passage are often formal affairs, requiring a lot of advanced planning and are steeped in social and cultural tradition. It is recommended that invitations for these events are sent out six to eight weeks in advance, especially if a formal dinner will be included.

Graduation Party

MR. & MRS. ANDREW FORMAN
INVITE YOU TO A BARBECUE TO CELEBRATE
THE SCHOLASTIC ACHIEVEMENT
OF THEIR SON ROBERT
GRADUATING FROM WILLIAM J. CLINTON HIGH SCHOOL
ON SATURDAY, JUNE 7,
AT 4 P.M.
AT 58 HOLLAND ROAD
WILKES-BARRE, PENNSYLVANIA

KINDLY REPLY BY JUNE 1ST
570-555-9162

Cotillion or *Quinceañera* (Parents Hosting the Event)

Mr. and Mrs. Ronald Robins
Invite you to a small, private dinner-dance
in honor of their daughter
Graciella Elyse
on Saturday, the fifth of April,
at seven in the evening

The Oak House
9872 Appleton Street
St. Petersburg, Florida

The favor of a reply is requested by March 21, 2014

The reply cards for each of these events would follow the same formula as discussed earlier in the chapter. If the cotillion or *quinceañera* is being sponsored by a group or organization, and several girls will be making their social debut at the same function, the invitation could alternately read "the annual debutante ball" instead of naming the debutante specifically.

INVITATIONS TO CHILDREN'S PARTIES

Invitations to birthday and other parties for young children that fall outside the realm of rites of passage can have a theme that matches the party theme, but they should be simple. When preparing and sending your invitation, even for the youngest of socialites, it is important to be aware of the lead time. Chances are your children and their friends are being invited to the same parties and events, and that every family, just like yours, has multiple obligations and social commitments.

Child's Party

> **Please join Sara-Beth
> for cake and ice cream
> at her
> Fifth Birthday Party
> at 2 P.M., on Saturday, November 2, 2013
> at the Frey's
> 1249 Morning Glory Lane
> Brookline, Massachusetts**
>
> **R.S.V.P. 617-555-0119**

Child's Party Alternative

Jason's Turning Five!
Join us for cake and ice cream
at 3:30 P.M.,
on
Saturday, November 9, 2013
at the Johnson's
1249 Morning Glory Lane
Brookline, Massachusetts

R.S.V.P. 617-555-5540

USEFUL WORDS AND PHRASES

We invite you to share our joy

✻

Please join us

✻

I/We request the pleasure of your company

✻

I/We request the honor of your presence

✻

Join us for the happy occasion of...

✻

Announces

✻

Reception to follow

Luncheon to follow

✳

...is called to the Torah

✳

Join us in celebrating

✳

Join us in bearing witness to

✳

...as Jonathan makes his First Communion...

✳

...as Jonathan is Baptized, Confirmed, et cetera...

✳

Invite you to celebrate...

✳

Cordially invites...

✳

You are cordially invited to attend...

✳

The favor of a reply is requested by...

✳

R.S.V.P.

✳

Please reply by (with the reply date)

✳

Regrets only

⇌ Chapter 4 ⇌
Acceptance and Regret

LETTERS OF ACCEPTANCE

Letters of acceptance can be used for social and business occasions. For social events, they should be used when a formal reply is required, but reply cards are not included in the invitation. For a social occasion, you can use your card or note stationery to write a simple note to the hosts. The note should match the same level of formality as the event.

For business events, they should be used to confirm or accept arrangements in writing. In business situations, e-mails and memos are both appropriate because of the speed and timing with which business decisions are made. However, even if you are sending a letter of acceptance in a memo or e-mail, you should use business format.

Writing a Letter of Acceptance

For business situations, when sending the letter of acceptance in the mail, use letterhead or quality bond paper and type the letter of acceptance. For social situations, you can use your personal stationery and either handwrite or type the letter of acceptance.

Format the letter with your address (unless using letterhead), the date, and the recipient's address. Use the active voice, be brief and sincere, and don't write more than one page. Thank the reader for the invitation and be specific about the details for which you are accepting the invitation or arrangements. Tell the reader that you are looking forward to the event or whatever it is that you are accepting. End with a complimentary closing, followed by your name and signature.

Business-related Letter of Acceptance

Dear Anthony,

Thank you for inviting me to speak at the "Moving Forward" symposium in February. I just want to confirm that the meeting is scheduled for Wednesday, February 5, through Friday, February 7, 2014, at the Hyatt Regency. My presentation on building a business identity will be approximately 30 minutes long, with additional time for a question-and-answer period with the audience. I look forward to receiving more details from you about the event particulars. Please let me know which type of audio-visual or multimedia equipment will be available.

I am looking forward to hearing from you and to working with you once again.

Yours sincerely,

Jules Madison

Jules Madison
Madison Associates

Letter of Acceptance for a Social Event

Dear Mr. and Mrs. Robins,

Thank you for the kind invitation to your dinner and dance for Graciella Elyse on Saturday, April 5. Roberto and I are happy to attend and are looking forward to watching little Graciella make her debut.

Very sincerely yours,

Alicia Sullivan

LETTERS OF REGRET

As with letters of acceptance, letters of regret can be used for both social and business situations. They are a polite way of informing the recipient that you are unable to attend or cannot make the commitment or respond positively to the offer implied in an invitation. They can also be used to counter an earlier acceptance of an invitation or commitment if a more pressing matter precludes your attendance. If this is the case, you should inform the person you're writing to as soon as you know that you cannot attend or participate.

Writing a Letter of Regret

As with letters of acceptance, follow the same guidelines for letters of regret. For business situations, use letterhead or quality bond paper and type the letter of acceptance. In many cases, using e-mail is also appropriate but should still follow the format of a written letter. For social situations, use your personal stationery and handwrite or type the letter.

Letters of regret that are responding to an invitation should match the formality of the invitation or arrangements. Format the letter with your address (unless using letterhead), the date, and the recipient's address. Use the active voice, be brief and sincere, and don't write more than one page. Thank the reader for the invitation and be specific and sincere about your regrets. In the letter, express that you wish you could attend or participate. If you would like, give a brief explanation for why you cannot attend, but you are not required to. End with a complimentary close, followed by your name and signature.

A Business-related Letter of Regret

Dear Anthony,

Thank you for inviting me to speak at the "Moving Forward" symposium in February. I am honored that you thought of me as a possible speaker. Unfortunately, I will be traveling most of February and cannot be a part of this year's program. Please let me know if there is any other assistance that I might be able to provide, or if I can suggest another colleague who might be available to present. Please do not hesitate to call me at 202-555-9984 to discuss.

Kindest regards,

Chantal Burnhardt

Chantal Burnhardt
Burnhardt, Murray and Zink Associates

Social Letter of Regret

Dear Mr. and Mrs. Robins,

Thank you for the kind invitation to your dinner and dance for Graciella Elyse on Saturday, April 5. Unfortunately, Cecil and I are unable to attend the event in honor of Graciella because we have our niece's birthday party that same day. Please tell Graciella congratulations, and we hope to see you all soon!

With sincerest regrets,

Gertrude Robertson

USEFUL WORDS AND PHRASES

Thank you for the invitation

✳

I am writing to accept...

✳

I look forward to...

✳

I/We are happy to attend/share this occasion...

✳

Thank you for including me/us

✳

I regret to inform you that I will be unable to attend...

❧ Chapter 5 ☙

Congratulations

WRITING CONGRATULATORY LETTERS

Written congratulations can be used to accompany a gift or to commemorate any significant life event, achievement, or milestone. Commercial greeting cards and personal stationery can be used for notes and letters of congratulations in personal situations. In business situations, both letterhead and commercial greeting cards are acceptable. Write from the heart and be sincere. Use the active or passive voice. When writing, format your note in semi-block format, including your address, the date, and the recipient's address. Start by offering congratulations, making sure to include what you are congratulating them for. Include well wishes, such as for continued success, a long life together, or happiness.

In the end, the goal of a congratulatory letter is to share sentiments for good health, wealth, success, and longevity, and to praise the honoree's accomplishments and goals and revel in their happiness.

Letter of Congratulations Examples

Dear Angela,

I heard about the great news of you passing the Boards. I am so proud of you, but I know that it cannot compare to how proud you are of this wonderful achievement, especially after such hard work. Congratulations and may you have many more successes and blessings throughout your medical career!

With love,
Aunt Margaret

Dear Greg and Jane,

Let me begin by saying congratulations on your recent engagement! I heard the news, and I am so excited for you both. How wonderful that you've found each other, and I wish you both a lifetime of happiness.

All my love,
Christine Larson

USEFUL WORDS AND PHRASES

General Congratulations

It's true—good things do happen to great people!

*

Celebrating success! Celebrating you! Congratulations.

*

Thank you for letting me share your joy!
Happiness shared is delight doubled.

*

Enjoy the love, laughter, and limelight
that are yours today.

*

May the happiness you're feeling
today go on and on and on.

*

Bells! Whistles! Fireworks! Well done!

*

Envisioning a dream is easy.
Seeing it through is not!

*

I'm overjoyed. It couldn't have
happened to a nicer person.

*

Three cheers from me to you on your triumphant day!

I'm so happy for you. You deserve nothing but the best.

∗

You are proof that dreams and possibilities are
endless when you believe in yourself.

∗

No one deserves success more than you!

∗

Whatever you've been doing, keep doing it!

∗

I'm delighted about your news!
You truly earned this success.

∗

You deserve a round of applause
for a job well done!

Graduation

A cap. A gown. A diploma.
A whole new chapter in the story of you.
Congratulations!

∗

Wishing you adventure, success, and
happiness for all your tomorrows.

∗

May I make an educated guess?
You're the brightest and the best!

We are so proud of your accomplishments—
in the past and, especially, today.

*

I'm so pleased for you! Now it's time to show
the world how brightly you shine.

New Job, Promotions, and Retirement

You're a success looking for a chance to happen!
Congratulations on the new job.

*

You've always been one step above the rest.

*

Good luck with your promotion.

*

A new job, new friends, new challenges—good luck!

*

Business brought us together, but friendship has kept us
close. Here's to you, a wonderful associate and friend.

*

I always knew you'd go far—clearly, I'm
not the only one to recognize this.

*

You've helped your family grow and prosper.
Now it's time to relax and enjoy the results.

*

Now it's time to really work hard—at enjoying life, that is!

Engagements, Weddings, and Anniversaries

What greater joy can there be for two souls than to know
they are destined to be together? Congratulations!

∗

I'm so glad to hear that you're tying the knot!

∗

Sparkling stone. Sparkling future. Congratulations.

∗

Life looks kindly on those who love and bestows special
blessings on those who join their hearts.

∗

Here comes the bride! Happy engagement!

∗

May today be the beginning of
a lifetime of beautiful days.

∗

May your love grow with each passing day
as you create the life of your dreams.

∗

It is not enough to wish you happiness in your life together.
I wish you a lifetime of days even happier than today.

∗

May your wedding day be just the beginning of a
new life overflowing with warmth, laughter,
connection, friendship, hope, and love.

May the two of you forever be blessed
with all that makes you happy!

*

Nothing is better than good old-fashioned love.
May yours see a ripe old age.

*

Here's to happiness: May it fill your life always!

*

May your love begin with "Once upon a time…"
and blossom into "happily ever after."

*

Best wishes to you both on your wedding day.

*

It's a day you'll remember forever.
Treasure it as I treasure both of you.

*

Let love lead the way through your life together.

*

May every tomorrow be twice as sunny and
sweet as all the days that came before.

*

Wishing you more love with every year you share.

*

The best way to enjoy life is to savor the passing of time.
Let's celebrate another year together.

Your life together is an inspiration.
Happy anniversary!

*

The honeymoon still isn't over!
Happy anniversary.

*

May your lives continue to be blessed by love.

*

Here's to many more beautiful years together!

Expecting a Baby and Births

I heard you've got a special delivery on the way.
Congratulations!

*

Babies are little miracles with a whole lot of "kick."
Congratulations on your pregnancy.

*

A few months from now you'll discover that you
can do three things at once and that moms really
do have eyes in the back of their heads!

*

Wishing you a happy, healthy bundle of love.

*

May your new baby bless your life
with joy and happiness.

May today be the beginning of
a lifetime of beautiful days.

✳

How wonderful that you're adding
more love to the world.

✳

May you savor the sweet joys of parenthood.

✳

The sounds of baby feet will soon fill your home with
unimaginable love and infectious laughter. Enjoy!

✳

When a child is born, parents are too.
Congratulations!

✳

May your new little one be as healthy
and happy as he [or she] is beautiful.

✳

What could be nicer than a new baby to love?
Congratulations!

✳

A baby is life's greatest blessing.

✳

May your new baby boy [or girl] open
your eyes to all that's beautiful in life.

✳

⇜ Chapter 6 ⇝

Get Well Soon

Letters and short notes can lift someone's spirit when they're suffering or recovering from a prolonged illness, an accident, or a surgery. If you cannot visit them, a get-well-soon note could be more appreciated than flowers.

Get-Well Letter from a Friend

Dear Mitch,

I heard from my mother the other day that you recently had knee-replacement surgery. And to think, you were always the invincible one during all those years playing hockey together! Now we have something else in common. I've had a few issues with my knees as well, as I'm sure Mom told you. If you want to talk, don't hesitate to give me a call. I am glad to hear that the surgery was a success, and I'm sure you'll be back on your feet (and probably back on the ice) in no time. Between Beth and Dr. Morris, you couldn't be in better hands. Wishing you a speedy recovery, and we'll have to see how that new knee of yours holds up on the ice the next time I'm in town.

Always and fondly,

Pete

Your note should be handwritten on personal stationery or in a greeting card. Be sincere in your expression for the person's well being and let them know how you heard about their situation if they did not tell you. Do not use get-well notes as a platform to discuss your own ailments. If you can appropriately offer genuine assistance, either emotionally or in person, go ahead. Consider the personality of the person you're writing. Sometimes a humorous approach is the perfect way to bring a smile to someone's face. An illness can mean many hours spent alone in the hospital or at home, and a funny letter can lift spirits that may be dampened by feelings of sadness and grief.

USEFUL WORDS AND PHRASES

I hope you are feeling better soon.

＊

Sorry to have heard about your illness/surgery.

＊

Best wishes for a speedy recovery.

＊

Here's wishing you a speedy recovery!
We miss you when you're not here.

＊

Get better soon—there is still much joy ahead of you!

＊

Sorry to hear you've been ill.

＊

Wishing you a short stay and a speedy recovery.

✦ Chapter 7 ✦
Sending Sympathy

When just the right words are needed, it's often the hardest to find them. Loss and grief are universal emotions, but they are also very personal. People sometimes wonder whether it is better to not say anything so as not to further upset the person in need of sympathy. But by acknowledging another's pain or difficulty, you can help them work through it. It also lets the person know that he or she is not alone, and at the very least, that someone is thinking of them, praying for them, or sending them well wishes.

When writing a letter of sympathy, think of the kinds of things that you would want to hear from others. Remember that offering sympathy is not about you, it is about the recipient. However, it's good to be mindful of the person's personality and how they tend to handle things. If, for example, they tend to be vague about issues, then you should be vague, too. For example, when discussing cancer, some people say, "the C word" instead of calling it by name. Therefore, if they are grieving for someone who has lost the battle, you shouldn't say, "I'm sorry that Jack's cancer took its toll." Instead, say something like "I am sorry for your loss." On the other hand, if they are open about sharing, you can be just as forthright in your choice of words. Know that as long as what you write is from your heart and sincere, it is bound to be beautiful.

Many think that the only time to offer sympathy is for death or grave illness. But life's journey has so many ups and downs, and the low points are when people need the support of their friends and family to get through them. These periods include job loss, divorce or separation, coping with illness, a bad breakup, or any other negative or unpleasant situation. But don't let this list limit you. If you feel the need to express your caring, empathy, or sympathy for another, go ahead. A sympathy letter can be a simple random act of kindness that elevates the spirits of someone who is down.

A sympathy letter should acknowledge the person's emotional state, whether it is pain, anguish, sorrow, or anger. Share your empathy—your deep understanding of the situation with a personal anecdote. If you haven't personally been in that same situation yourself, and therefore cannot add a personal anecdote, explain how you can only begin to imagine what it is like to be in their situation.

Offer emotional assistance when realistically possible and appropriate. Don't pledge support that you have no intention, desire, or ability to uphold should the person accept your offer. This may sound harsh, but it really isn't. Some people think, "Well, everyone knows that it's just what you say, but nobody ever takes you up on it." Not true. A person who is in pain just might reach out to grab that emotional lifeline you've offered, and in writing no less. To suggest that there is no limit to your time or availability is insincere and unfair to them and to you. Instead, you can add words of encouragement and hope that can help the person through the difficult period they are in.

Remembering people who have suffered a loss in the past is also important. The holidays, birthdays, and anniversaries can be difficult times for people who are in a state of distress. They are often reminders of what they have lost when it seems that everyone around them is filled with joy. In these situations, timing is critical. If you know that someone's birthday is approaching, make sure that you send your greeting so that it arrives on or before the person's birthday (or the birthday of the person that has died, if that is the case). Doing so will help the recipient through what may be a recurring period of difficulty and sadness. Christmas, Hanukkah, and Thanksgiving are critical periods. If the person is suffering from grief related to military service, their own or a loved one's, whether tragic injury or death, don't forget them on Memorial Day and Veteran's Day.

In her *Guide to Excruciatingly Correct Behavior*, Miss Manners gives examples of what not to say to the bereaved. This list can include anyone who is in a state of despair, not just those who are mourning the death of a loved one. This list includes but is not limited to:

* It's all for the best.

* He /She wouldn't have wanted you to grieve.

* He/She wouldn't have wanted you to cry.

* Do you think you ought to be going about like this—so soon after...?

* You can always have more/other children.

* You're young, smart, handsome/pretty. You can remarry.

* Don't you think it's too early to...

* At least you had many years together. It's not like what happened to me.

Most of those statements imply some unsolicited judgment about how the person is handling a tragedy. On the surface, they seem well intentioned, but they are really in poor taste. Unless the person asks, or they are in need of protection or intervention, keep your opinions to yourself. Don't try to diminish their situation by talking about your own. That's not what is meant by the suggestion to empathize by showing that you understand. The focus should be on the person in pain and not on you. Remember that sympathy is not about you. It's about the person in pain. You can offer the personal story as an anecdote to let them know that you have been there, but don't use their grief as a platform to discuss your own situation. The simple way to approach this is to say, "I know what you're going through, and I've been through something similar." You can then offer your ear or shoulder for support with a statement such as, "If you want to talk or hear how I got through it, let me know. I'm here for you."

HOW TO WRITE IT

Sympathy letters should be handwritten on personal stationery or typed on personal letterhead. They can also be handwritten in a blank or trade greeting card in addition to the sentiment printed in the card. Use semi-block format and include your address, the date, and the addressee's address. Write from the heart. Start by acknowledging the person's grief, sorrow, or pain and how you learned about it. Express your sympathy next and offer words of kindness.

Death/Condolence

Dear Margaret,

I was so sorry to hear that your father has died. And I am sorry that I could not attend the funeral. Your father was such a wonderful man, and I have such vivid memories of him coaching the girls' softball team. He was always so encouraging and hysterically funny. He could turn even the worst game into something positive.

I wish you much comfort, peace, and many happy memories of him to get you through this difficult time. My thoughts and prayers are with you and your family.

Your friend,

Julia

Anniversary of a Sad Event/Birthday of Deceased

Dear Marcia

How are you? I just wanted to write to let you know that we're thinking of you. We know that this is a difficult time of year with Paul's birthday approaching for the first time since his death. Know that we love you very much and that you are always near in our hearts and thoughts, even if we are miles apart.

Lovingly,

Barbara

Miscarriage

Dear Sandra,

Jack told me about your miscarriage, and I am so sorry for your loss. I know how excited you both were, and I also know what you are going through—Matthew and I were there a few years ago. If you need someone to talk to, or just need some additional companionship during this difficult time, let me know, and we can get together for tea. Matthew also offers the same for Jack, since it's not easy for the father either. Just know that you have a lot of support, and that you are in our thoughts and prayers.

Very sincerely,

Ellen

Divorce/Separation/Breakup

Dear Jonah,

The second I heard about your separation from Julie, I had to write. I can only imagine how hard it is to have plans to build a life together suddenly change, especially after moving halfway across the country to do so. Please know that George and I are here for you to help in any way that we can. You have a lot of friends to support you through this difficult time. We will help you get through it so that you can have the happiness you deserve.

Sincerely,

Mary

Military-related

Dear Bill,

I've been thinking about Zach a lot lately. Perhaps it is because Memorial Day is approaching. I realize that this must be a difficult time for you and Margaret, and I wanted to share my thoughts of how proud I am of Zach for serving our country and giving the ultimate gift. Zach was always a fine boy, and you raised him to be such a good, upstanding man. I am sure that as a soldier, he was no less than a brilliant and true leader.

It is not easy losing a son, and I am sure that though every day may get a bit easier, it can still be difficult. Please know that my thoughts and prayers are with you today and always. May the happy memories of Zach and your pride in him bring you continued comfort.

Fondly from your dear friend,

Larry

These letters are only a few examples of the types of general social letters you can write to convey sympathy. The possibilities are endless. All you need is something to write about, something to write on, and something to write with. Don't forget to be sincere and write from the heart. A simple sympathy letter to a friend, relative, or coworker takes very little time and effort, but it could mean the world to the recipient.

USEFUL WORDS AND PHRASES

We are sorry for your loss.

✳

Our thoughts and prayers are with you.

✳

When your heart is empty, filling it with
happy memories can help.

✳

I am always here for you

✳

My heart aches for you.

✳

I was saddened to hear of your loss.

✳

Please know how very sorry I am.

✳

You are in my thoughts every step of the way.

✳

We hold you safe in our hearts
at this time of sadness.

✳

Know that I/we am/are here for you.

If I can help you at this time
of sadness, I am here.

✳

It's hard to understand why people are taken
from us, but find comfort in knowing you
were a special part of a well-lived life.

✳

Memories of love and friendship are
treasures to carry with you always.

✳

When the Lord calls our loved ones home,
he leaves a gift of memories in exchange.

✳

I'm here if you want to talk.

✳

Take heart. Time will soften the edges
and ease your burden.

✳

I cannot take away your pain, but I can
listen if you want to talk about it.

✳

Don't dwell too long on what
was or what might have been;
what will be is waiting.

⇒ Chapter 8 ⇐
I Love You...
Or Maybe Not

What could be more delightful than receiving a letter from your sweetheart? Writing one to your sweetheart. Love letters can help brighten, spark, and enliven a relationship, especially since many couples today are separated by hundreds or thousands of miles for weeks or months at a time because of military service, work, or school. Love letters don't need to be reserved for Valentine's Day (February 14) or Sweetest Day (the third Saturday in October). They aren't only for those couples who are geographically separated, either. You can send one to your spouse or boyfriend or girlfriend even when you live together. In your love letters, be sincere and speak from the heart.

Often, a love letter can do what spoken words cannot. You don't need to sound as lovesome as poet Elizabeth Barrett Browning, but you can still wear your heart on a sheet of paper—even if you cannot wear it on your sleeve. Letters can be short, but you want the person reading them to feel the same level of excitement and anticipation when opening and reading your letter as they do when they're with you. As with any letter, consider your audience. If your sweetheart isn't one for flowery phrases, skip them. Though the steamy, bodice-ripping love letter is probably not a good idea for new relationships, vague allusions to passion might be, especially if you are certain that no one else will read it. Beyond the standard rules of letter writing, there are no rules for sharing your love and sense of passion in a love letter. The only limits are the boundaries of your unique relationship.

HOW TO WRITE IT

Start by examining your relationship and your feelings about your significant other. Tell your sweetheart why you love them and what it is about them that makes you happy and in love. It's that simple. The format can be formal or informal, but it should be handwritten because it helps express the deep personal nature of the letter. Love letters are also a sweet addition to a greeting card.

Love Letter

> Dearest Meghan,
>
> Everything about you captivates me. When you look at me, I find it hard to speak and hard to think. I get lost in your eyes and in your laughter. With you, my soul leaps. I feel so special and honored that I am yours.
>
> With all my love,
>
> *Francis*

Sometimes, that's really all you need to write in a love letter to express your feelings. It doesn't have to sound like a romance novel, and it doesn't have to include every romantic thought you've ever had about your sweetheart.

USEFUL WORDS AND PHRASES

I love you.

✳

You mean so much to me.

✳

I'm so happy we met.

✳

You make my heart skip a beat.

✳

I truly enjoy the time we spend together.

✳

I can't wait until we see each other again.

✳

You bring me such joy and happiness.

✳

My world is brighter now
that you're in it.

✳

I'm counting the minutes
until I see you, my love.

✳

The best gift I've ever received is you.

Our love isn't a fairy tale—it's better. It's real.

*

The day I fell in love with you
was the best day of my life.

*

Your love is my most treasured gift.

THE "DEAR JOHN" LETTER

Paul Simon once sang "There Are 50 Ways to Leave Your Lover."
One that he didn't mention was *writing* your lover about it.
It's not a nice thing to do, but sometimes you find yourself in
a situation where you need to. "Dear John" or breakup letters
should be used as a last resort and when there is absolutely no
other way to dissolve the relationship. Be sincere and be direct,
but don't be mean. Don't use your "Dear John" letter as a forum
for telling your former love about all their worst traits and
habits. You want to break things off as smoothly as possible,
not wound your former lover or give them a reason to retaliate.
Be sensitive to their feelings and acknowledge that you are
sorry for the pain this may cause them. Keep the letter short
and to the point.

After you write your "Dear John" letter and before you send
it, sleep on it for a day or two. Then read it again and remove
anything that you think would be severely hurtful or that could
be misconstrued as a way out of breaking up. Put yourself in
the recipient's shoes—if you received your own "Dear John"
letter, would it cause you to react in an irrational way? If so,
rewrite the letter.

HOW TO WRITE IT

Similar to love letters, you should start by examining your relationship and your feelings. It is best to handwrite the letter unless the emotional gravity of the situation makes your penmanship difficult to read. Use semi-block format. Be candid but sincere. Begin the letter explaining why you are writing it. Be clear about the intentions of the letter. End the letter on a positive tone and wish the person well. Do not use "Love," for your complimentary close, as that will only confuse the reader.

Breakup Letter

Dear John,

Writing this is extremely difficult and painful for me. It is clear to me that we want very different things and that we are on different paths. You have been a great friend, and we have had wonderful and happy times together. But those happy times have given way to a relationship that is stagnant and unfulfilling—I think for both of us. I have decided that it is best that we no longer see each other. It will not be easy for either of us. Know that you will always have a special place in my heart and that I will cherish the good times we have had. Perhaps in time, as we both heal and grow, we may be friends again. But for now, I know that is not possible because it will be too easy to fall into our old patterns. I am sorry for any pain this may cause you, I just need you to understand.

Sincerely,

Mary

USEFUL WORDS AND PHRASES

I am sorry to do this in writing
instead of in person.

✳

Sincerely

✳

I can no longer be a part
of this relationship.

✳

I feel it's time for both
of us to move on.

✳

We are not in the same place with
this relationship anymore.

✳

I wish you all the best in the future.

✳

Though we have had
some wonderful times...

⇥ Chapter 9 ⇤
Writing While on Vacation

A fun thing to do while you are traveling is to send postcards or short letters from afar to friends and family back home. It lets them know that you are thinking of them, even if you're on vacation. You don't need to do this for a short weekend trip—unless you've taken one to some exotic or unusual location—but remember that your postcard may arrive long after you have returned home.

The body of a postcard or a short letter doesn't need to be too detailed. There isn't a lot of space on postcards anyway, so you need to be brief or write small (just don't write so small that the person reading it needs a magnifying glass). Keep in mind that postcards will probably get read by anyone who handles them, so choose your words carefully and with decorum. Write to your family and friends or close coworkers just to say a quick "hi" and to share some of the sights that you've seen or something interesting about the trip. Don't use postcards and notes-from-afar letters as a dig—as in "Ha, ha! I'm on vacation and you're not!" Be sincere and light. When writing to loved ones who are back home, don't forget to tell them that you miss them and love them.

If you're on a cruise or staying in a hotel, it is perfectly acceptable to use the stationery that is provided in your room or suite.

USEFUL WORDS AND PHRASES

Thinking of you...

✳

Wish you were here.

✳

I/We saw...

✳

The sights are amazing.

✳

You should come here on
your next vacation.

✳

I wish I could share this
experience with you.

✳

I hope this note finds you
with a happy heart.

✳

I know this would be a perfect
spot for your next vacation.

✳

We may be far apart, but you're
always in my thoughts.

❧ Chapter 10 ❧
The Holiday Letter

Some people prepare for the holiday season months in advance. They purchase the packages of greeting cards that went on sale immediately after Christmas last year. They have their database of names and addresses ready to print labels the day after Thanksgiving and will start signing their cards soon after that. Others have chosen the family photo and have placed their order with a photo-processing company and all that's left to do is click, pay, and send. For others who want to spread the holiday cheer, there is the holiday letter, the traditional end-of-year greeting that goes out to family and friends.

The holiday letter can be a thoughtful way to keep up with friends and family with whom you don't normally get to stay in touch throughout the year. The holiday letter is one way to stay in contact that is more personal than a signed "Season's Greetings" card. It eliminates the need to write personal notes in every single greeting card. Although that's a nice touch, writing personal notes on each one may take more time than you realistically have. You can, however, still write a personal note to selected people on your holiday letter.

Avoid sending the family holiday letter to business associates unless they are also close, personal friends. Business associates you do not know well may appreciate a holiday card, but when it comes to holiday letters, they may not be interested in your personal life or that your fifth grader won the school spelling bee. Also, be sure to mail your holiday letter early enough to avoid missing people who may be on vacation.

HOW TO WRITE IT

When writing the holiday letter, consider three things: timing, style, and audience. First, you want to ensure that your letter arrives on time for the holiday you are writing for. Hanukkah moves throughout the calendar each year, so pay close attention to that date. Kwanzaa is December 26 through January 1. While Christmas always falls on December 25, traditionally it is 12 days long; don't fret if the people on your list don't receive your letter by December 24. The New Year's holiday letter can be one way for both families and business owners to avoid the rush of the holiday season, gain some extra time to compose and send out their letters, and avoid the issue of offending anyone's religious or cultural preferences.

If you are sending your letter electronically, avoid sending it the last two weeks of December and the first three days of January since this is when most people are on vacation. This is especially important for businesses—there is nothing worse than getting back to the office on January 2 only to spend the first half of your workday sorting through e-mails.

Second, consider your family or business style when writing your letter and then determine whether you want the letter to include images from family or business events, a border, or other decorative motifs. Create bullet points for topics you would like to highlight. For a family holiday letter, you can organize the letter so you separately discuss each member of the family, or you can write about the family in general.

For a business holiday letter, you can call attention to the achievements the company made and goals for the coming year. Just be sure that this business information is safe to share with people outside of the company. Also be sure that you are writing a holiday letter and not giving an annual report, which is a separate document entirely. You may wish to thank your clients and colleagues for helping you achieve your goals and accomplishments. In both family and business holiday letters, extend your sentiments and wishes for your recipients to have a happy holiday season or a happy new year.

Third, your letter can be formal or casual in tone. Use the third person when referring to specific people if you want the letter to sound newslike. After all, the holiday letter is similar to a news bulletin or newsletter update. The format and design are not locked into any particular rules, but avoid using fonts that are too small or overly decorative, especially if you have a broad range of ages that will be reading it. What may be easy for you to read may not be for your 90-year-old grandfather.

Even if you use images and other embellishments, keep the rest of the letter simple. Also consider what kind of information is appropriate to share and what is not. That is, if you have a naturally open and candid personality, some of your readers may not. Be sure to adjust your tone and language so your letter is safe to read aloud to the six-year-old in the family so you don't find yourself blushing at the next family reunion.

Family Holiday Letter

Season's Greetings from the Smith Family!

Well, we've had quite a year and thought that we'd take a moment to highlight some of the bright spots with all of you. Mark started teaching again, taking a position with the local university as an adjunct professor. He is excited about it but is amazed at how unprepared his freshmen students are sometimes. He also loves that his work hours give him more time at home with Jane, Doug, and Michael as well as time for his writing.

After years of troupe leading and organizing local events, Ellen changed her volunteer status with the Girl Scouts to take on a paid position within the organization. Ellen is ecstatic about the new adventure and about getting paid to do things she was already doing. Plus, with Mark home more often and Jane in college, she needed something to occupy her free time.

Jane has survived her first semester at Stanford. She hasn't yet settled on a major and chides her father for his commentary about unprepared freshmen. She's also playing intramural soccer, is on the debate team, and is glad to be home for winter break to see old friends and eat food that doesn't require a meal card.

Doug and Michael are doing fantastic as well. The twins are inseparable as ever. Both took up hockey this year and are proving to be quite the players. We have

(Continued on page 104.)

no idea how they manage to find time to hang out with their friends and play video games. Oh, that's right—most of their buddies also play hockey, and when they're not on the ice they're in our den feeding their faces and playing those video games. At least we know where they are!

It's nice to have the whole family home for winter break. The house is louder and a bit messier, but it is filled with laughter and joy—even Rusty our dog seems to be enjoying all the commotion and holiday craze.

We hope you, too, are finding the joy and delight of family and friends. We wish you all a happy, healthy, and prosperous new year filled with many, many blessings.

Love,

Mark, Ellen, Jane, Doug, and Michael

Business Holiday Letter

Dear Colleagues and Friends:

As the holidays are a time to give thanks, we want to thank you, our clients and associates, for your business throughout the year. We would also like to take note of some of the highlights of this past year that could not have been possible without your support, encouragement, and patronage.

We were recognized by the Chamber of Commerce as one of the top growing businesses in the area. Matthew Platt and Geoff Laney became best-selling authors with their book on the industry, *The Story of Widgets: Industry Insiders Speak Out.* Overall, the company reached all of its benchmarks and was profitable in each quarter. As our gift to you, you will receive your very own signed copy of this best-selling book by mail to the address that we have for you on record.

We here at Laney, Laney, and Gherkin Widgets hope that you have a holiday season filled with cheer and that you have a successful, prosperous, and happy new year.

Yours,

Geoff Laney   Thomas Laney
Maria Gherkin

Geoff Laney
Thomas Laney
Maria Gherkin

USEFUL WORDS AND PHRASES

Wishing you all the happy things
this very special holiday brings!

*

'Tis the season to wrap the
world in joy and love!

*

Wishing you a sleigh full of wishes
and dreams come true.

*

May your heart be filled with every joy
during this special time of year.

*

Wishing you and your family a Christmas
frosted with winter magic.

*

Christmas is a special time of year, filled
with peace, love, and thankfulness.
Have a joyous season.

*

May the remembrance of the miracle
we celebrate bless your family
with hope and love.

May the blessings of Hanukkah brighten your life.

*

May the candles in your window
spark peace around the world.
Happy Hanukkah!

*

May the Festival of Lights shine bright with hope
and happiness this Hanukkah season.

*

May the principles of Kwanzaa offer guidance
and comfort to you and your family.

*

Celebrate culture and community, family and future.
Happy Kwanzaa!

*

Let the countdown to a memorable year begin!
Happy New Year.

*

At this joyous time of year, keep friends
and family close at hand.

*

Wishing you 365 chances to love, laugh,
and live your best year yet.

⇝ Chapter 11 ⇜
Thinking of You

A quick letter or note just to say, "Hi, I'm thinking of you" is a great way to brighten someone's day—especially those great friends that you were so close to but who are now sidetracked by responsibilities of work and family. We just don't have the same kind of time to spend with these old friends anymore because of other priorities or maybe geographical distance.

I know, you're thinking "What about e-mail?" Many of the suggestions given here can be used with e-mail correspondence as easily as they can with a note or postcard. However, there is something special about receiving a note in the mail. Chances are that the person you write to will be so happy to get something personal in the mail they'll want to open it right away.

Your letter doesn't have to be a long one. You don't need to tell your entire life story since the last time you saw each other. You can even use a greeting card to prompt you. There are a lot of "thinking of you" and nonromantic "missing you" cards on the market. There are also blank cards with great images that may be relevant to your personal history together. You can write inside the card itself, especially if it's blank, or you can use your note stationery and write a short letter yourself. You can also use special events, such as a birthday or anniversary of an event you shared together as a reason to write. In the end, you really don't need a reason at all. Old friends and family members alike will be delighted to get this random act of kindness from someone special—you!

HOW TO WRITE IT

These types of letters can be handwritten or typed. Using semi-block format, arrange your letter starting with your name and address, followed by the date and the addressee's name and address. Start with "Dear [person's name]" followed by a comma. Start the first paragraph with something like "How are you?" and then tell the person why you are writing and what made you think of them. Maybe share personal stories and anecdotes. Keep the tone conversational. At the end, invite the person to write back to you and include a complimentary closing followed by your name and signature. Don't forget to sign your letter if it's typed.

Letter to an Old Friend

Dear Beth,

I was at the store today picking up some things for the kids. I turned down the wrong aisle and ended up in the card aisle, where I saw this card. It made me think of you immediately.

So, how is everyone? I can't believe that it's been so long since we saw each other. Things here are well. The major news to report is that Melissa lost her front teeth. She's growing up so fast!

I'm going to keep this short, but I hope to hear from you soon. Kisses all around!

Love,

Sandy

Letter to a Family Member

Marian McGeorge
7447 Maple Street, Apt. 7F
Jacksonville, FL 32099

Dear Aunt Marian,

How are you? I wanted to write a quick note to say "hello" and to let you know that I am thinking of you. I know that we don't get to see each other very often, but you are always in my thoughts and heart. Peter hopes to see you in the summer again, and he still talks about the fun he had at your house during our last visit—especially playing with Snowpuff. He calls all cats Snowpuff now. It's terribly cute, but it always warrants an explanation to new people. I've enclosed a couple of recent pictures of little Peter for you. You'll be amazed at how much he has grown. He has locks of curls just like cousin Jeff—it's uncanny! I guess they skipped me and went straight to Peter.

I hope that you enjoy all of the pictures. We will arrange our calendars and plan another family trip to see you soon. Of course, you are always welcome at our home as well!

With love,

Dawn

See how easy that was? Sometimes a few paragraphs and a sweet anecdote or two are all you need for an uplifting note to brighten anyone's day.

USEFUL WORDS AND PHRASES

How are you?

*

I was just thinking of you.

*

We may be far apart, but you're
always in my thoughts.

*

I'd love to know how you're doing.

*

Sharing with friends makes life
much more fun. Please write.

*

I miss you.

*

"Wish you were here" just doesn't
express how much I miss you.

*

I was just counting my blessings,
and you came to mind.

＊

Thoughts of you always
make me smile.

＊

I hope this note finds you
with a happy heart.

＊

Through your letters, I hear your
laughter. Please write soon.

＊

Looking forward to
hearing from you.

＊

→ Chapter 12 ←
Anger and Apologies

Letters written in anger can be therapeutic for the writer. You can get all of your rage and fury out on paper and avoid other ways of mismanaging your temper or mishandling a situation. Hate mail and angry letters should rarely be sent. Go ahead, though, and write the letter. Allow it to be long and ramble on to get out all of your frustration. Do not, however, send it.

It is important to let the letter rest—put it down and sleep on it for a day or two. Then take the letter out and reread it. Try not to get angry all over again and consider why you were angry in the first place. If there are key issues or topics that need to be addressed, leave those and delete any personal attacks or curse words. Then go back over the key points and try to address them clearly and succinctly so that your letter is not longer than two pages. Consider how you would feel if you received such a letter and give that same courtesy to the person you are writing. Remember that they may have no clue that you are angry with them or that they have done something so displeasing that you need to write them about it.

If, after you have edited your original letter, it turns out that you are willing to speak to the person, use the letter as a guide for talking to them. If you are still too upset to talk to the person, let the letter sit for another day and repeat the process until it is lucid and no longer than two pages.

If you still need to send the letter, go ahead and send it. But be prepared for the consequences, and don't forget to destroy the original rant.

HOW TO WRITE IT

Think about why you are angry. Be direct, candid, and sincere. Do not be mean or rude. Use the semi-block format for your typed or handwritten letter. Remember that the reader may not realize you are angry. Explain why you are disappointed or angry. If there is some action that you need from the reader—such as to stop doing something—tell them so in a firm but polite manner. Use terms such as "I feel" and "I believe" when describing what the person did to make you angry. You can close your letter with "Sincerely," or "Respectfully," depending on the circumstance.

USEFUL WORDS AND PHRASES

I am sorry to do this in writing instead of in person.

✳

I am frustrated by...

✳

This is difficult to say, so I am writing you instead.

✳

I want to tell you that something has been bothering me.

✳

Please understand that I don't hate you, but...

✳

When you [insert action], it makes me feel [insert emotion].

Angry Letter

Dear Samantha,

I am writing you because I have to get something off of my chest. At this point, I am not sure if I can discuss it with you in person yet.

I am really irritated by the way you constantly flirt with my boyfriend. We've known each other for many years now, and you are a great friend. But whenever all of us are together and there is a guy present, even if the guy is with someone else, you turn into a completely different person.

I am confident in my relationship with Sean, so it's not that you are a threat, just a distraction, since guys can't seem to resist your hair twirling, eye batting, constant touching, and other flirtatious things that in any other situation you would never do. I need you to stop. Whether you stop doing it with others, I don't care. But when it comes to Sean, please stop. You can be friendly, but the overly flirtatious behavior with him has to end. I know that you are a caring friend, a true friend, so I know that you will be able to do this small thing for me and will understand where I'm coming from.

Sincerely yours,

Tammy

APOLOGIES

In 1976, Elton John sang, "Sorry seems to be the hardest word." But it doesn't have to be. Apologies can go a long way to mend a relationship that has been fractured. That's not to say that it will heal everything, but at the very least, it will let the person you've offended know that you acknowledge that you have hurt them, whether intentionally or accidentally. There are two kinds of apologies: the ultra sincere kind where you are as devastated for hurting someone as they are hurt, and the social apology where you realize that it is best to keep peace by extending the olive branch and acknowledging your infraction whether or not you thought you were wrong.

The key in an apology is realizing that it is not about you. It's about the person to whom you are apologizing. In some instances, you can offer ways to make amends. Or better yet, just do it. Do not go into writing an apology letter expecting immediate forgiveness or reconciliation. Depending on how deep the wound is, it will determine if and when forgiveness is granted. Once you've extended the apology, the outcome is up to the recipient. Consider the kind of apology that you would want were the shoe on the other foot. Be sincere even if you're writing a social apology. Most people who know you well will read right through insincerity.

HOW TO WRITE IT

Use personal stationery or a greeting card to handwrite your apology. Use semi-block format and include your address, the date, and the addressee's address. Keep the apology brief but directly say what you are apologizing about. That way, the recipient will know that you realize what you did and that what you did hurt or offended them. Use the active voice and where possible, offer to make up for your actions. Close your letter by restating your apology along with "Sincerely yours," followed by your name and signature.

Sincere Apology (in response to Tammy's letter written in anger)

Dear Tammy,

I got your letter. I'm writing because after reading your letter, I figure that you are still too upset to talk to me. I was wondering why we hadn't seen each other lately. I had no idea that I've been causing you so much distress. Please know that I would never intentionally do anything to come between you and Sean, and I am so very sorry that my behavior seemed inappropriate. I thought that I was being fun and friendly, and I guess I went over the line. When I think about it, I probably would be angry too if the tables were turned. Maybe we could come up with a signal or code word or something, so that if I start getting out of control like that again, you can let me know. I'd hate to think that I'd done something to cause a rift in our relationship when we've been such great friends for so long and have been through so much together. I hope that you can accept my sincere apology.

Give me a call when you're ready and maybe we can get together—just us girls, even if you're still unsure. I love you!

Very sincerely,

Samantha

From Samantha's letter, you can tell that she was caught off guard not only by Tammy's letter, but also by the fact that she was doing something that hurt her friend. She responds by acknowledging her friend's anger and what she did to offend Tammy, and is sincere in doing so. She also offers a way to mend the situation but gives Tammy enough space to reconnect in her own time. Given how upset Tammy was, chances are that she will not be expecting a letter of apology. By receiving one from Samantha that is sincere and acknowledges her need for space in dealing with the issue, she may find her feelings softened.

Social Apology

Dear Mr. Beck,

    I am really sorry that my friend Mike broke the windshield of your car when we were playing baseball at my house on Saturday. I realize that since Mike was my guest, I am responsible for his actions. I hope that by offering to rake the leaves and mow your lawn for the next three weekends it will make up for the cost of a new windshield. I sincerely hope that you are not upset with my parents or me anymore.

Sincerely, your neighbor,

Billy Adams

In this letter of apology, Billy probably doesn't think that he should have to do anything to make up for something that he didn't actually do. But he also has an end goal—he doesn't like that there is negativity between his family and his neighbor, so he offers an apology and a method of recompense. Even if Mr. Beck doesn't take Billy up on his offer, Mr. Beck will probably be touched that Billy thought about it—even if it was prompted by his parents.

USEFUL WORDS AND PHRASES

I am very sorry.

*

I didn't realize that...

*

I'm sorry that I hurt you.

*

I apologize for causing you pain.

*

I will try to do better.

*

Please understand...

*

I hope that you can forgive me.

Please accept this heartfelt apology.

✳

Please accept this sincere apology.

✳

I am sorry to do this in writing
instead of in person.

✳

I didn't realize how
much I hurt you.

✳

I sincerely hope you know
this was not intentional.

✳

Our friendship means the world
to me, and I hope this does
not come between us.

✳

You have a special gift for listening
with your heart. I hope we can
eventually get past this.

✳

When I count my blessings, our friendship
tops the list. Nothing would mean
more than your forgiveness.

＊

This has been a learning experience
for me, and I hope I never
have to repeat it.

TIPS

Do

* acknowledge the person's feelings.

* directly apologize for what you have done
  or how you have hurt them.

* be sincere and write from the heart.

* offer to make up for your actions if the
  situation warrants it.

* ask for forgiveness if the situation warrants it.

Don't

* discount the person's feelings

* make excuses for yourself or your actions.

* make false promises.

* write an angry or hurtful letter as a response.

⇶ Chapter 13 ⇜
It's All Business

Our overflowing mailboxes at home are evidence that business letters don't just come to you at the office. Letters come to us daily regarding an array of issues: banking, credit cards, insurance, medical issues, solicitations, and more. Even though you're at home, the rules of business writing etiquette still apply. After all, you are corresponding with a business, so your end of the conversation should be as professional and businesslike as possible.

You don't need to be in business to know how to professionally present your written word. The skill of writing an efficient business letter (even if you are not a business professional yourself) is key in getting your needs met and your voice heard. Competent business writing increases the probability of a situation being handled effectively and expediently. Some appropriate situations for writing a business letter are when handling banking, lending, and investment issues, medical issues, insurance issues, tax issues, and dealing with contractors and service providers. Within this group, the appropriate scenarios for using a business letter include but are not limited to making requests for information or a particular service, making changes in service, updating personal information, reporting a complaint, and making a commendation.

When writing your personal business letters, use quality stationery and make sure your letter is typed out and not handwritten. Letters should be formatted in block or semi-block style and single-spaced between lines and double-spaced between paragraphs. Before writing your letter, make sure that you have the correct names and titles of anyone in the company who is relevant to the situation. Be sure to include key information such as account, reference, or invoice numbers. This makes it easier and faster for the company to access your file or account. However, never include your social security number, employer identification number, or tax identification number unless it is absolutely necessary. With the rise in identity theft, you do not want to give that information to potential thieves just in case your letter falls into the wrong hands.

THE PAPER TRAIL

If you're wondering why you should write a letter or send an e-mail regarding a personal business matter instead of picking up the phone, it is because of the paper trail. Anyone who has seen popular court-related reality shows knows that without proper documentation, all you have is a series of "he said, she said," which will solve nothing, especially if it turns into a legal issue or ends up in litigation.

Documentation provides a chronological record of the events of the issue, which is important for you and whoever is involved in addressing the issue. If you send a letter by mail, always make copies of your original signed letter. You can also scan it and save it to disk. If you send an e-mail, make sure you are saving a copy to your Sent folder. If you work in an office, do not use your company's business stationery for your personal business unless your company is acting on your behalf. In that case, there is probably a staff member who will handle the letter, so make sure that person has all of the relevant information needed and that you receive copies of any letters written on your behalf.

HOW TO WRITE IT

Be direct and firm but not caustic or aggressive. Be sure to address only the relevant information needed for handling the issue by using short, clear sentences. Your business letters should be no longer than two pages. In your closing, thank the recipient for their time and attention to the matter and include the best way they can contact you during business hours. If additional documentation is required, be sure to include that as well.

If a business matter relates to working directly with a person or group of people from the company, find out who the person's supervisor is so that you can inform them of your positive or negative experience. Be sure to briefly describe what the person helping you did and include all relevant dates of interaction—especially if they were helping you with a matter over a long period of time. If you don't know the person's name, be extra detailed in sharing the times and dates of your interaction. Chances are the company has records of who worked when and will be able to match that with the information you provide.

The following examples show a variety of home-based business-related issues. The same writers are used for each letter to illustrate how many home business situations there are.

Financial Letter, Including Changes of Name and Address

Janet B. Lawson
514 Maplewood Circle
Appleton, WI 54913

October 25, 2013

Elizabeth Cormier
Account Manager
Big Investment and Annuity Firm
P.O. Box 0000
Chicago, IL 60611

Re: The Big Bank and Trust Company
    Annabelle J. Smyth
    Acct. No. ABC0000

Dear Ms. Cormier,

I am writing as a beneficiary of my grandmother's account and instructing you and The Big Bank and Trust Company to send the remaining shares assigned to me to my current address: 514 Maplewood Circle, Appleton, WI 54913.

Please note that at the time of the last disbursement of shares as my grandmother's beneficiary, I was not yet married. It is likely that your records list me under my maiden name, Janet Elizabeth Bryce. It is also likely that the address of record is my address prior to my marriage, 5 Winchester Road, Evanston, IL 60202.

(Continued on page 126.)

I have included a copy of my marriage certificate to prove that the identities of Janet Elizabeth Bryce and Janet B. Lawson are one and the same. If you need any additional information, please do not hesitate to contact me at 920-555-2904.

Many thanks in advance for your assistance with this matter.

Very sincerely yours,

Janet B. Lawson

Janet B. Lawson
Beneficiary of Annabelle J. Smyth

Encl.

Medical Insurance Letter

Janet B. Lawson
514 Maplewood Circle
Appleton, WI 54913

February 5, 2015

Big Medical Insurance Company (BMIC)
P.O. Box 1000
Milwaukee, WI 53201

Re: Group Number: 00000
    Contract Number: 123456789
    Policy Holder Name: Alan G. Lawson
    Patient Name: Samuel Bryce Lawson
    Issue: Billing for Well-baby Appointments

To Whom It May Concern:

We have received several bills from University Hospital Pediatrics regarding well-baby appointments and vaccinations for our son, Samuel Bryce Lawson. We have two medical insurance policies with BMIC through my company and my husband's company. After speaking with Marilyn G., a representative from BMIC regarding our coverage, we learned that our first coverage with Major Accounting Firm, LLC, does not cover these appointments. However, our second coverage through the University of Wisconsin does. We understand that when the first coverage is rejected, the issue usually gets bumped to the second coverage. In our case, it

(Continued on page 128.)

did not, as I learned when I spoke to Sandy B., a BMIC representative in the department that handles University polices. We were instructed to send the explanation of benefits letters (which are enclosed) so that the issue can be rectified, since our son's well-baby appointments and vaccinations should be covered by our plan with the University.

If you have any questions, please do not hesitate to call us at 920-555-2904. Thank you in advance for your expeditious assistance with this matter.

Yours Sincerely,

Janet B. Lawson

Janet B. Lawson

Tax-Related Financial Issue

Alan G. and Janet B. Lawson
514 Maplewood Circle
Appleton, WI 54913

September 27, 2014

Discovery and Tax Enforcement Division
P.O. Box 8949
Madison, WI 53708-8949

Re: Notice of Proposed Income Tax Adjustments
for 123-45-6789 and 987-65-4321

To Whom It May Concern,

We are writing to disagree with the adjustments made to our 2013 Wisconsin Tax Adjustment. We spoke with a Treasury Representative prior to the original due date for the response and were informed of the documentation that we needed to provide, part of which we did not receive from the originator until after the deadline. Because of this, it was impossible to reply before September 17. We are responding now, at the first opportunity and immediately upon receiving the needed documentation for our rebuttal.

We disagree with the adjustments made to our 2013 Wisconsin Tax Adjustment for the following reasons:

1. The $134.00 proposed tax was already paid.

2. The wages earned, $3,356, for which those taxes were assessed were not earned in the state of Wisconsin.

3. The wages earned, $3,356, for which those taxes were assessed were not earned by a resident of the state of Wisconsin at the time.

4. The applicable taxes on those wages were paid to the state in which they were earned, Illinois.

Documentation and Reasoning:
The $3,356 (actual amount was $3,356.88) was earned during the month of January 2013, the only month that Janet B. Lawson (then Janet Elizabeth Bryce) earned wages

(Continued on page 130.)

from Northwestern University in 2013. At the time, she was still a resident of Illinois, and she did not move to Wisconsin until February 1, 2013. She earned no more wages from Northwestern University after January 31, 2013.

The 2013 W-2 was missing because it was sent to the address-of-record with the Payroll Department at Northwestern University. (Copy of 2013 W-2 from Northwestern University attached.) After speaking with the Payroll Department to obtain a copy of the 2013 W-2 form, it was determined that even though Janet Elizabeth Bryce had updated her address with other departments of the University, the W-2 went to her former (Illinois) address at the beginning of January 2014. By this time, any U.S. Postal Services forwarding orders to her new Wisconsin address had expired. The former address was 5 Winchester Road, Evanston, Illinois 60202. Furthermore, the wages were earned prior to her marriage to Alan G. Lawson in July 2013. (Copy of State of Wisconsin Certificate of Marriage and Marriage License are enclosed.)

Thus, according to the copies of the 2013 W-2 form as provided by Northwestern University, you will see that as a single wage earner at the time the wages were earned (by a resident of Illinois at the time the wages were earned), that in fact, $143.36 was paid to the state of Illinois. Thus, the correct state to which taxes were and should have been assessed is Illinois. We owe neither the proposed tax of

$134 nor the interest of $30.00 for a total of $164.00 to the state of Wisconsin for the wages of $3,356 because said wages were neither earned in Wisconsin nor by a resident of Wisconsin living as a nonresident in another state.

As per the instructions on the notice that we received, a copy is also enclosed. Please correct our record. If you have any questions regarding this matter, please do not hesitate to contact us at 920-555-2904.

Many thanks for your time and assistance.

Respectfully yours,

Alan G. Lawson

Janet B. Lawson

Alan G. Lawson and Janet B. Lawson

Encl.

Despite advice against doing so, the previous letter does include the social security numbers of the couple. In this case, it is perfectly acceptable because social security numbers, employer information numbers, and tax identification numbers are the equivalent of account numbers and how the Internal Revenue Service identifies people for tax-related matters. Additionally, the letter to which they were responding included their social security numbers and the instructions stated to include those numbers on any correspondence regarding the matter.

Change of Service Letter

Alan G. Lawson
514 Maplewood Circle
Appleton, WI 54913

March 25, 2014

Big Medical Insurance Company (BMIC)
P.O. Box 1000
Milwaukee, WI 53201

ATTN: Ms. Frances Hansen, Policy Holder Customer
Service Liaison

Re: Confirmation of service change for contract
     number 123456789

Dear Ms. Hansen:

Thank you for your assistance regarding adding
my wife, Janet B. Lawson, to my policy. Though the
human resources department at Big Major Accounting
Firm did have the forms that I submitted for the
significant-life-events benefits change, my wife is
still not listed. As per your instructions, below is
the information and supporting documentation to
ensure that the change is reflected in my account
and its corresponding records.

• Group number: 012345

• Policyholder name: Alan G. Lawson

- Contract number: 123456789.

- Added beneficiary: Janet Bryce Lawson. Date of birth: June 5, 1968

- Effective date of change: March 10, 2014

- Copy of marriage license is enclosed as documentation.

Thank you for your continued assistance with this matter. If you need to reach me during business hours, please call me on my mobile phone at 920-555-3332.

Yours sincerely,

Alan G. Lawson

Alan G. Lawson

HANDLING CONTRACTORS

When having work done on your house such as an addition or renovation, it may involve working with contractors and subcontractors no matter how big or small the project.

Although contracts with the company will be signed, it is still important to place any key communications with your contractor in writing—and that means a business letter. From the initial agreement through the final punch-list, putting requests, notifications, and changes in writing protects both you and the contractor you are working with. It also helps maintain a professional business relationship with the contractors no matter how friendly you may become during the course of the project.

Using the Lawsons as our continued example household, the following letters can be applied to other general home-related business situations as well.

Confirmation of Services Letter

Alan G. and Janet B. Lawson
514 Maplewood Circle
Appleton, WI 54913
920-555-2904

May 12, 2014

Paul Diamante, Owner
Additions and More
7360 Great Lakes Avenue
Appleton, WI 54913

Dear Paul:

It was a pleasure meeting with you and discussing the additional 255-square-foot room that will be built on the east end of the first floor of our house, as well as the necessary renovations to the existing infrastructure to make all parts of the house up to present code. This includes changing our fuse box to a circuit breaker, updating the plumbing on the first floor to accommodate the half-bath that will be placed in the aforementioned room, proper insulation, and HVAC issues.

The new room will have a foundation built as well, and the renovation to the master bedroom will include a walk-in closet and connecting breezeway to the small bedroom adjacent to the master bedroom. The 255-square-foot room on the first floor will also have three skylights, built-in shelving units, and hardwood floors to match the hardwood that is throughout the existing structure. With all the renovations, you agree to use energy-efficient technology wherever possible.

Designs will follow the original concept that Alan and I created, modified per our meetings with you based on your building and construction expertise. We understand that work will commence on June 1. Prior to that date, we will make the necessary adjustments to our living space to accommodate when ground will be broken, walls knocked out, and the new and old structures united.

Payment for the project will be remitted as follows: one-third upon signing (done at our May 11 meeting); one-third halfway through the project; one-third at the end of the project.

We are pleased that you and your team will be working on our renovation project, and we look forward to working with you over the coming months.

Very sincerely yours,

Janet B. Lawson

Janet B. Lawson

Change in Service Letter

Alan G. and Janet B. Lawson
514 Maplewood Circle
Appleton, WI 54913
920-555-2904

July 26, 2014

Paul Diamante, Owner

Additions and More
7360 Great Lakes Avenue
Appleton, WI 54913

Re: Design change for walk-in closet

Dear Paul:

Thank you for the wonderful work that you have been
doing. I want to confirm the changes that we discussed
yesterday for the walk-in closet. Because of considerations
about the style of the doors and how they open, they affect
what will become the passage to the adjoining room, which
will become a nursery. Instead of accordion folding doors
for the closet, we would prefer the doors to be pocket
doors. We realize that will entail restructuring the wall
to be able to create the "pocket," and this will add both
time and labor costs to the project. Please e-mail me the
projected increases and the new timetable.

Sincerely yours,

Janet B. Lawson

Janet B. Lawson

Many letters dealing with contractors are simply to make the entire process more simple and clear for both parties. The letters are straightforward ways of exchanging information. Complaint letters, on the other hand, present information on what has happened and explain the reason why you are dissatisfied. As with hate mail, if you are angry when composing your letter, be sure to wait a day before looking at it again. Allowing yourself to get all of your frustration out on paper can be therapeutic, but will not necessarily generate the kind of response you seek. By waiting a day before sending the letter, you will be able to read it with more objectivity and less emotion. After you have slept on it for at least a day, edit and remove anything that could be interpreted as offensive or as a personal attack on the recipient.

Though you may think that an angry letter will elicit a quick response, it may only create more problems in the process. You want to voice your frustration in a useful and tactful way that will make the reader see that you mean business but that you are not a loose cannon.

Complaint

Alan G. and Janet B. Lawson
514 Maplewood Circle
Appleton, WI 54913
920-555-2904

August 3, 2014

Paul Diamante, Owner
Additions and More
7360 Great Lakes Avenue
Appleton, WI 54913

Dear Paul:

Overall, we are pleased with the work that you have
been doing on the renovations and are looking forward
to begin furnishing the addition downstairs. However,
as I mentioned during our phone call, we have an issue
with one of your subcontractors.

The group that you sent to lay the parquet in the new
room has not completed the job as anticipated or as Alan
and I discussed with you. There are several issues that
concern us. First, the threshold between the new room
and the existing house is uneven and does not match
the other thresholds on the level. Second, some areas are
already buckling and need to be replaced. The bottom
panel of one of the built-in units is marred and will need
to be replaced.

We would like to have these issues rectified now rather
than wait for them to be rectified when it comes time to

do the punch-list. When asked when they were returning, John D. told me that they had finished the job. According to my assessment, they have not. Please have them return to take care of these unresolved issues as soon as possible. If you wish to discuss this further, I can be reached on my mobile phone at 920-555-3443. I have enclosed photos of the areas mentioned.

Many thanks in advance for your prompt attention to this matter.

Sincerely yours,

Janet B. Lawson

Janet B. Lawson

Encl.

Unfortunately, most of us decide to pick up the pen when we are dissatisfied, want to file a complaint, or when responding to a letter initiated by a business. Complaints are the norm but commendations and praise rare. However, you can change that with your business letters. Since customer satisfaction is often one of the top priorities for companies, why not let them know when you are satisfied? It can go a long way to let a company know when you receive stellar service or a situation is handled effectively.

If the service relates to working directly with a person or group of people, find out who the person's supervisor is so that you can inform them of your positive experience. Be sure to briefly describe what the person helping you did. Also include relevant dates of interaction if they were helping you with a matter that was handled during an extended period. If you don't know the person's name, be as accurate as possible in sharing the times and dates of your interactions. Chances are highly likely that the company has records of who worked when and will be able to match them with the information you give. If you receive stellar service, go ahead and let the company know with a written letter.

Letter of Praise/Commendation Letter

Alan G. and Janet B. Lawson
514 Maplewood Circle
Appleton, WI 54913
920-555-2904

September 4, 2014

Paul Diamante, Owner
Additions and More
7360 Great Lakes Avenue
Appleton, WI 54913

Dear Paul:

Thank you again for the excellent work that you and your team at Additions and More did on our home renovations. We have received so many compliments from friends and family members about your work.

Thank you for your honesty every step of the way and for addressing issues with the greatest sense of professionalism and consideration.

Mike and Larry were always on time, worked hard, and were respectful of our personal space. And with the exception of the one incident—which was rectified almost immediately—your subcontractors were equally professional and courteous.

Please know that we will be more than happy to refer you to anyone that we know who is looking to make home improvement changes.

Very sincerely yours,

Janet B. Lawson

Janet B. Lawson

❧ Chapter 14 ❦
School Time

It can be difficult for parents to decipher when it's appropriate to correspond with teachers and school administrators. Many parents want to give their children a certain level of independence and teach them responsibility, but it's important to know ways you can be involved with academic and school-related correspondence and when it should be your child's responsibility. This section involves questions directed to teachers as well as letters from students to teachers and from parent-volunteers to parents.

LETTERS FROM PARENTS TO TEACHERS

Establishing communication between parents and teachers is essential for ensuring that a student's needs are met. Telephone calls are not optimal either for a number of reasons. Unless a teacher has given parents his or her personal contact information, the best time to call is probably during school hours, which is also when they are teaching. Phone calls from teachers can sometimes yield unpleasant responses from parents caught off guard, and from there communication can go downhill. E-mails or short letters and notes between parents and teachers, however, can be effective.

INQUIRIES ABOUT GOALS AND EXPECTATIONS

There are a variety of reasons for parents to write to teachers and administrators. When fostering a community of learning that actively involves the teacher-parent-student triad, letters and short notes can pave the way for open and respectful communication. Don't just rely on flyers and school billboards for announcements and pertinent information.

HOW TO WRITE IT

Using personal stationery or letterhead, set this letter in block or semi-block format and write in the active voice. The tone can be formal or informal, but it should not seem too casual if an informal tone is used. You want to show the school or teacher that you are interested in understanding their goals and expectations in a way that is authoritative but not forceful or threatening.

Goals and Expectations Inquiry

Robert and Elizabeth Petersen
291 Drake Circle
Bellinghamton, WI 53562
September 7, 2013

Ms. Julia Lardie
Freshman Guidance Counselor

Bellinghamton Senior High School
351 Lincoln Road
Bellinghamton, WI 53562

Dear Ms. Lardie,

We are concerned about the courses that our daughter, Sarah-Beth, is taking this year. It seems that none of the

(Continued on page 144.)

classes on her freshman schedule are college-preparatory classes. We know that she tested well and had excellent grades throughout elementary and middle schools, so I am sure that you can understand our concern that the classes on her schedule are not going to prepare her adequately for college work. We hope to schedule a meeting with you in person to discuss Sarah-Beth's schedule and the goals and expectations for her as a freshman. We would like to arrange a meeting as soon as possible so it does not become too late to have her schedule changed and so she does not fall behind in the more advanced classes. I can be reached at 606–555–9781. Thank you for your time and attention, and I look forward to hearing from you.

Sincerely yours,

Robert Petersen

Robert Petersen

NOTES REGARDING BEHAVIOR AND GRADES

Waiting until there is a severe problem is too late; instead, it is a good idea for parents to contact teachers and administrators about brewing issues when the issue is first brought to your attention. The letter should be more of an alert to the teacher or administrator that there seems to be an issue and that you would like to discuss it. Avoid making assumptions about the teacher's or administrator's awareness of the situation with your child before speaking with him or her—especially if it is a situation that involves another student. Stress that your concern is with meeting your child's best interests and how you as a parent can work to meet those expectations with the teachers or administration.

HOW TO WRITE IT

Using personal stationery or letterhead, set the letter in block or semi-block format. Use the active voice and a formal, but not forceful, tone. For such important matters, type the letter instead of handwriting it. Start the letter by informing the instructor or administrator of the problem. Express sincere concern and request a meeting with the teacher or administrator (or both) to discuss the issue in person. Include the best way to contact you so that the meeting can be arranged. End with a complimentary close and your signature.

Letter about Behavior and Grades

Robert and Elizabeth Petersen
291 Drake Circle
Bellinghamton, WI 53562

December 1, 2013

Malcolm Roberts, Sophomore History Department
Bellinghamton Senior High School
351 Lincoln Road
Bellinghamton, WI 53562

Dear Mr. Roberts,

Thank you for your note. My wife and I agree that the sophomore year of high school is a very important year

(Continued on page 146.)

and that Josh's midsemester report card was quite disappointing. His grades are clearly below where they should be. We are also concerned about what you described as his frequent disruptions.

We agree that Josh is not meeting his potential, and we would like to set up a meeting with you to discuss it. I work from home and can meet with you during the day. We can also set up an evening appointment if you wish to meet with both Elizabeth and me. Perhaps early next week would be a good time since it will be right before the winter break, which we might be able to use to our advantage.

We can be reached at 606–555–9781 and look forward to hearing from you soon.

Yours sincerely,

Robert Petersen

cc: Andrew Murray, Principal

Letter about Behavior and Grades

Robert and Elizabeth Petersen
291 Drake Circle
Bellinghamton, WI 53562

November 4, 2013

Dr. Elayne Stockington
William H. Lincoln School
Bellinghamton School District
351 Lincoln Road
Bellinghamton, WI 53562

Dear Dr. Stockington,

Our youngest son, Chad, is a sixth grader in Mr. Kay's homeroom. Chad has brought to our attention that some eighth graders have been harassing sixth-grade students.

Through discussions with other parents it seems as if this has become a regular occurrence. Apparently each week this group of eighth graders seeks out some sixth grader to persecute, and then these sixth graders get in trouble when they are only trying to defend themselves, while the eighth graders remain unpunished. We wish to discuss this situation with you and Mr. Kay as soon as possible and would like to set up a meeting in person. We can be reached at 606–555–9781. Thank you in advance for a timely response.

Respectfully yours,

Robert Petersen *Elizabeth Petersen*

Robert Petersen and Elizabeth Petersen

USEFUL WORDS AND PHRASES

Bring to your attention

✳

I hope we can work together to...

✳

I look forward to hearing from you.

✳

I appreciate a timely response.

✳

Want to inform you

✳

Want to remind you

✳

best interests

✳

academic success

✳

disruptions

✳

tardiness

✳

absences

✳

I'd like to set up a meeting

✳

goals

performance

＊

ability

＊

aptitude

＊

encourage

＊

suggest

＊

potential

＊

SCHEDULING A MEETING OUTSIDE OF REGULAR PARENT-TEACHER CONFERENCES

Sometimes a parent or guardian might want to meet with a teacher outside of regularly scheduled parent-teacher conferences, such as if there are questions or concerns about a child's progress, workload, or assignments. Because the best time to call a teacher is during school hours, which is when they are teaching and many parents are working, an alternative is to send the teacher a letter to the school by mail. Do not send the letter to school with your child, though. It's best to mail the letter directly to the school to be sure it arrives.

HOW TO WRITE IT

On personal stationery or other quality paper, draft your letter to the appropriate faculty or staff member, and use block or semi-block format. You can handwrite or type the letter, and try to keep it brief. Use the active voice and choose the formal or informal tone depending on your personal preference. Include as much information as possible. State your concern, issue, or reasons for wanting to meet. Inform the teacher of your availability and provide your contact information and the best time and way to reach you. End with a complimentary close and signature.

CONCERNS AND COMPLAINTS

No teacher or administrator likes to receive angry letters. It is important for parents and guardians to remember that there is a person on the other end of that letter, especially because it's difficult to not be emotional when it comes to our kids. Letters are better than phone calls in these situations because writing the letter gives you a chance to get your ire out before putting it in the mail. You can let the letter sit for a day or two, or keep the e-mail in your "drafts" folder before clicking "send."

HOW TO WRITE IT

Be sure to address only the relevant information needed to have the issue handled by using short, clear sentences. Explain why you are dissatisfied, and present only the facts that led to your disappointment. Don't be accusing or make personal attacks on a teacher or staff member. If you are angry when composing your letter, be sure to wait a day before looking at it again. By waiting a day before sending the letter, you will be able to look at it with more objectivity. After you have let the note or letter sit, edit it and remove anything that could be interpreted as a personal attack on the recipient. End with a suggestion to meet in person, your contact information, and a complimentary close and your signature. When typing the letter, do not type in all caps or use bold and italics for emphasis, and be sure to proofread it one last time before sending it.

Letter to Request a Meeting Along with a Complaint

Geoffrey Sullivan
727 Oxford Road
Bellinghamton, WI 53562

December 5, 2013

Mr. Albert Payne
William H. Lincoln School
Bellinghamton School District
351 Lincoln Road
Bellinghamton, WI 53562

Dear Mr. Payne,

I would like to schedule a meeting with you to discuss Sarah's homework. I find it odd that she never seems to have any. Sarah says she completes it before school ends—sometimes before class ends—because it is so easy. I am a little concerned that she may not be challenged enough, and I'm wondering what we should be doing at home. I work from home and can be reached there on most days.

If you are available after school on Wednesdays, I can meet with you then. My number is 606–555–9712. I look forward to hearing from you soon.

Sincerely,

Geoff Sullivan

Geoff Sullivan

Notice how this letter was very simple and straight to the point, even though he was communicating a complaint to his daughter's teacher. Keeping things professional as opposed to emotional and angry in a letter will make a teacher or administrator more willing to discuss such concerns with a parent.

USEFUL WORDS AND PHRASES

challenge

*

progress

*

achievement

*

I look forward to hearing from you

*

I would like to discuss...

*

I hope to schedule a meeting to...

*

I hope you are available to...

*

resolve

improve

✳

disappointed

✳

unsatisfied

✳

I have a question about...

LETTERS TO TEACHERS FROM STUDENTS

Sometimes a student might want to write to their teacher or instructor. There may be various reasons, from wanting to thank them for something, scheduling a meeting to discuss a grade, or wishing to start a club or organization. If you are in school and under 18, inform your parents so that they are aware of the situation—this will protect you and the teacher.

HOW TO WRITE IT

On personal stationery or other good paper, draft your letter to the appropriate faculty or staff member and use block or semi-block format. You can handwrite or type the letter. Use the active voice and choose the formal or informal tone depending on your personal preference. Be sure to state the specific reason for wanting to meet. Inform the teacher of your availability and suggest meeting when you are free during school hours, during their office hours, or briefly after school. End with a complimentary close and sign the letter.

Letter to a Teacher from a Student

Geoff Sullivan, Jr.
727 Oxford Road
Bellinghamton, WI 53562

December 13, 2013

Mr. Malcolm Roberts
Bellinghamton Senior High School
351 Lincoln Road
Bellinghamton, WI 53562

Dear Mr. Roberts,

Thank you for your help with the sources for my history paper. I'd also like to meet with you about a couple of things. First, I'm interested in taking the AP history class next semester and wanted to know what you think and if I would succeed in this class. Second, a few of us have been thinking about starting a history club and wanted to know if you'd be our faculty advisor. I have fourth period free on Tuesdays and Thursdays, and I'm usually free on Fridays immediately after school. I hope that you'll be available to talk soon, especially since I would like to finalize my second-semester schedule before winter break. I'll touch base with you after our next class.

Sincerely,

Geoff Sullivan, Jr.

Geoff Sullivan, Jr.

USEFUL WORDS AND PHRASES

touch base

✻

I look forward to hearing from you.

✻

I would like to discuss...

✻

I would like to schedule a time for us to meet regarding...

✻

I hope you are available to go over...

✻

I have a question about...

✻

I appreciate the comments you made on my project, and I would like to meet with you in person to discuss them in further detail.

✻

I cannot thank you enough for counseling me on choosing a college. You really helped make my decision easier!

NOTES FOR OUTINGS AND FIELD TRIPS ORGANIZED BY PARENT-VOLUNTEERS

Advanced planning is crucial when alerting parents and guardians about possible outings and field trips. As with any other invitation to an event, parents and guardians should be given enough time to respond and decide if their child can or should participate, and they need all the information about the proposed outing.

HOW TO WRITE IT

Include information about possible cost, lunch arrangements, the location, times and scheduling, method of transportation, the purpose of the outing, and how it relates to the curriculum or extracurricular activity. Also include a permission slip and a due date for its return with the parent or guardian's signature and any fees that should be collected in advance. If the trip or activity is a relatively expensive one, be sure to include information about any financial support that might be available for families and the deadlines for applying.

Using school letterhead, set in block, semi-block, or memo format. Use the active voice. Describe the trip or activity using a formal or informal tone.

Field Trip Note

William H. Lincoln School
Bellinghamton School District
351 Lincoln Road
Bellinghamton, WI 53562

February 10, 2014

Dear Fourth Grade Parents and Guardians,

As part of the Social Studies unit on Government, we are planning the annual fourth grade trip to the state house in Madison. Students will get a tour of the state house and have the opportunity to meet and speak to Representative Alan Swenson, our district representative. Last year's trip was a great success, and we are grateful to Rep. Swenson for making time in his schedule to meet with us again.

The trip is planned for March 20, 2014. Students should arrive at school on time and report to homeroom where attendance will be taken. From there, the classes will assemble in the gym for a head count and announcements at 8:20 A.M. We expect to start boarding the buses at 9:00 A.M., and we plan to leave the school at 9:15 A.M. We expect to arrive at the state house at 10:00 A.M. We will return to the school at 3:15 P.M. Students should dress warmly and bring their lunch and an afternoon snack with them, along with a notebook and pens or pencils.

Please note that everyone will need to go through the security checkpoint and all bags will be examined. It is also imperative that you return the permission slip by the deadline, as we need to provide security at the state house with a list of the names of every child and adult participating in the trip beforehand. The trip schedule and permission slip are enclosed. Please sign and return the enclosed permission slip no later than March 1, 2014.

If there are any parents who wish to chaperone, please call Mrs. Danbury, field trip coordinator, at the school office at 608–555–2300 ext. 15.

Sincerely,

Jane Bernstein *Georgia Sollars*

Jane Bernstein and Georgia Sollars
Fourth Grade Parent Volunteers

Encl: permission slip, itinerary

CC: Mrs. Pat Serbinsky and Ms. Ellen Baer
Fourth Grade Teachers, William H. Lincoln School

❧ Chapter 15 ❧

Organizations

From intramural sports teams to parent teacher associations, you or your children may be part of many different organizations. Sometimes, you as a member may need to write to the leadership. In other instances, you may be the organizer who is reaching out. In this chapter we'll cover a few common scenarios.

NOTES FROM PARENTS TO ORGANIZATIONS AND ADMINISTRATORS

Starting an Organization

Most schools and school systems have a variety of parent-led organizations, from Band Boosters to the Parent Teacher Associations (PTA) or Parent Teacher Organization (PTO). When trying to establish an organization at your school, first do background research well in advance of approaching the school with the idea. After you have done the necessary research, contact the school administration to see what the correct channels are for starting a club or organization. Present a sound plan for the organization or group, including its function and purpose, duties, projected expectations from the school in terms of participation and support (whether financial or otherwise), and expectations from members. Make sure that you have provisions in place for fundraising, bylaws, and other organizational and administrative issues.

Write a cover letter to the administration about your idea, and set up a meeting to discuss it. If you have support from other parents in the school, let the administration know and perhaps meet as a group with the administration to find out what additional action may be required on your part.

HOW TO WRITE IT

Using personal stationery, letterhead, or good quality bond paper, type your letter as a business letter using block or semi-block format. Address the letter to the principal or administration. Start by introducing yourself, your idea, and why it is important for the school community. Outline your goals and objectives and how you plan to implement the program, including who will do what in the organization, what your bylaws will be, and other relevant information. In your letter, request guidance and support from school administration. Provide your contact information and end with a complimentary close and your signature. Don't forget to provide any supporting documentation that you may have, including information from a parent organization, business plan or articles of organization, and any financial information. While this all seems very formal, presenting a professional image will let the administration know you are serious.

Letter for Starting an Organization

Marybeth D'Mitruchina
17 Pleasant View
Bellinghamton, WI 53562

April 23, 2014

Ms. Johanna Haynes, Assistant Principal
Bellinghamton Senior High School
351 Lincoln Road
Bellinghamton, WI 53562

Re: Band Booster Club

Dear Ms. Haynes,

Band is such an important part of the lives of many students and families, and we would like to start a band booster club at the school. Because there are many costs beyond what the district provides in order to have a quality band program, as a booster club we want to work to defray these costs and reduce the fees that each family needs to pay toward their student's music education. Volunteer parental involvement and support are key when it comes to providing the support and encouragement for every student to reach their highest level of success.

The booster club would allow us to provide support for all aspects of the Bellinghamton Senior High School Band Program, including the marching band, symphonic and jazz bands, and the chamber ensembles. We already have a list of parents and members of the community interested in participating in a band booster club at all levels of organization. We have drafted a set of bylaws and proposed meeting times, and have started conversations with Mr. Johnson, head of the music department, who is very interested in seeing a band booster club at the school.

We see the band booster club as an organization of adults interested in supporting the music programs at Bellinghamton Senior High School. The band boosters hope to raise money through fundraising and assessments. The booster leadership—the primary group of parent organizers—will develop the booster budget with input regarding where the funds will be allocated. We believe that each family who has a child in any of the band programs will be considered a member of the boosters.

I hope that we can count on you and the rest of the administration to help us realize this dream. Please let me know what the next steps are in the process to officially start a BSHS Band Booster Club. Perhaps we can schedule a meeting with the other parents interested in organizing the booster club and Mr. Johnson in the coming weeks. I can be reached on my cell at 606–555–6412.

Thank you in advance for your time.

Sincerely yours,

Marybeth D'Mitruchina

Marybeth D'Mitruchina

CC: Mr. Bruce Johnson, head of music department
    Mr. Andrew Murray, Principal

USEFUL WORDS AND PHRASES

purpose

✻

We are proposing...

✻

We would like to start...

✻

We envision...

✻

Our goals and objectives are...

✻

We hope that you will be a part of...

✻

We hope that we can count on the administration to...

✻

We hope that you will support our endeavor...

✻

articles of organization

✻

Bylaws and constitution

implement

*

We look forward to hearing from you.

*

fundraising

*

We believe this organization/club will
benefit the students because...

LETTERS OF INTRODUCTION FROM COACHES AND GROUP LEADERS TO PARENTS

Coaches and group leaders—such as conductors for the band, orchestra, or choral groups; youth-theater directors; Scout leaders; and youth-group leaders—should introduce themselves to parents and guardians before the start of the season or program. Parents welcome these letters and appreciate what to expect and what's expected of them so there are no surprises down the road. Taking the time to do this helps pave the way to a good relationship with the parents of the children who will be in your care.

Use the opportunity to explain your policies or those of the parent organization thoroughly, the goals for the season or group, and the schedule for practices, meetings, games, or outings. Remind parents and guardians about registration deadlines and other things for which they are responsible. Include any helpful tips that you as an expert can provide.

HOW TO WRITE IT

Using personal stationery or regular letter-size paper, choose block, semi-block or simple format. Type your letter. Introduce yourself to the readers and tell them a little about your background and expertise with the club, sport, or group. Outline your plan for the season or session as well as your goals. Include dates, times, and any other important information that parents will need. You can include those as separate enclosures. If possible, give them information for how they can check that information online as well, in case they should lose the enclosures. Provide parents with your contact information, and close the letter by expressing your excitement about the program. End with a complimentary close and your signature.

Introduction to Parents from a Coach or Group Leader

Frances Best
33 Clinton Road
Arlington, MA 02474

August 20, 2014

Dear Flash! Team Members and Parents,

The fall soccer season is starting soon, and I am excited about the start of the U-12 Girls Soccer Season. Most of you already know each other and me from previous years, as most of our team has stayed together. We have two new team members this year, Jacqui and Allison, who have both moved to the area recently. Welcome, Jacqui and Allison!

Practices will be on Tuesdays and Thursdays from 3:30 to 5:00 P.M. at Lambert Field. Practice starts promptly at 3:30 P.M. The first official practice will be Tuesday, September 9. Please make sure the girls arrive dressed appropriately for soccer practice with cleats, socks, and shin guards. Goalies should bring their gloves. Please don't forget sunscreen and water for your player. If anyone is available and would like to have a preseason practice to go over drills, I am free on August 30 and September 6. We should be able to get the fields without competing with preseason football practice. Please let me know of your interest by August 15, so I can alert our team manager, Mrs. Dorton, so that she can secure a field. (Many thanks once again to Mrs. Dorton for volunteering to be the team manager!)

As always, here are a few reminders:

- No jewelry during practices or games, per ASC and MYSA rules.

- Per MYSA and FIFA rules, there is a zero-tolerance policy for parents addressing referees.

- Uniforms will be distributed during practice before the first game.

- Our practice and game schedules can always be found online at the Flash! Facebook page. Notifications of time changes or cancellations will be sent by text message and by e-mail, so please make sure we have accurate contact information on file.

(Continued on page 166.)

- We will have the official game schedule by the end of the first practice. Games are scheduled to start the first Saturday in October.

- Players should not wear cleats on the pavement because it degrades the cleats for optimal play. Wear sneakers or sport sandals on the pavement.

I hope everyone had a wonderful and fun summer and is pumped up for another great soccer season! We will be collecting and confirming e-mail addresses and phone numbers after the first practice, and a full calendar will be distributed once we know the game schedule. See you all at the first practice! If you need to contact me, my cell phone number is 781-555-9132. Go Flash!

Sincerely yours,

Coach Franny

Coach Franny

USEFUL WORDS AND PHRASES

Looking forward to the...

✳

The season begins on [date].

✳

Welcome!

Our goals and plans for this year...

✳

Don't forget that you will need to provide your own _____.

✳

Practices will be held every _____.

✳

Uniforms [or equipment] will be handed out on _____.

✳

Those who need rides can contact _____.

LETTERS FROM PARENTS TO COACHES AND GROUP LEADERS

Unlike school-related situations, the opportunity to have face time with coaches and group leaders may be greater, since these activities tend to occur outside normal school and business hours. For minor things, you don't need to put it in writing. However, there are times when you will want to, such as when you have a planned absence or the child is otherwise unable to participate in the regularly scheduled activities. Remember that while your situation is important to you or your child, the coach or group leader has several people to keep track of. They can only remember so many things—so put it in writing. A short note should suffice. Also remember that many coaches and group leaders are volunteers, so while they may be fully engaged when it comes to that activity, they also have their own families and work on their minds as well. Writing a short, informal note not only ensures that they have the information that they need, it is a kind thing to do.

HOW TO SAY IT

Use personal stationery and handwrite or type the letter, or use e-mail if that is the coach's preference. Keep the note simple and use the active voice. The format can be semi-block or simple. Explain or describe the issue thoroughly, and request a meeting, if it's appropriate. Remember to provide your contact information if necessary, and end with a complimentary close and your signature.

Letter from Parents to Coaches and Group Leaders

Dear Coach,

We just wanted to remind you that Hillary will not be at next Saturday's game because we will be out of town for a family wedding. We will be back for practice the following Tuesday. Hillary will leave her gloves with Lisa in case a substitute goalie needs them.

Sincerely,

Michelle Emerson

Michelle Emerson

USEFUL WORDS AND PHRASES

I want to remind you that...

﹡

I'm writing a quick note to...

﹡

I want to let you know...

﹡

inform

﹡

touch base

﹡

I am writing to thank you for such a successful season. The children couldn't have done it without you!

﹡

⇻ **Chapter 16** ⇺
Letters of
Recommendation

Whether you're requesting letters of recommendation for a job, internship, or college application, or writing a recommendation yourself for a student or colleague, this chapter has you covered with tips and examples.

REQUESTING LETTERS OF RECOMMENDATION

When requesting a letter of recommendation from an instructor, employer, or colleague, do it in writing even if you have spoken to them about it beforehand. Because it is important for your recommendation to focus on your academic talents and accomplishments, your request letter will give the person a concrete reminder of these things and about teaching you or working with you—especially if it has been a while since they did. And make sure to send a thank-you note afterwards!

HOW TO WRITE IT

Give your recommendation writers at least one month before letters are due. If you have preprinted forms, provide them to the people writing your recommendations, along with a stamped envelope addressed to the institution. Be sure to double-check the directions on the admissions application to see whether the institution wants the letters to arrive separately or with your entire package.

Recommendation Request Letter

Alexis Young
874 Boylston Street
Bellinghamton, WI 53562

September 24, 2014

Mr. Sam Priebe
Bellinghamton Senior High School
351 Lincoln Road
Bellinghamton, WI 53562

Dear Mr. Priebe,

Since Physics was one of my best classes last year, and you asked me to participate in various after-school experiments for your research, I hope that I can ask you for a letter of recommendation for my college applications. I'm not sure if you know, but I am taking AP Physics this year.

I realize that you are very busy, which is why I am asking you so early in the school year. I have narrowed my list to seven schools—four schools that I really want to attend next fall, one difficult school, and two safety schools. I have recently begun assembling the application materials. If you are able to write a recommendation, I will provide you with all of the required forms and information after I have had my official meeting with the guidance counselor.

I have a free block during fifth period this semester and can touch base with you then if you don't have a class at that time. My parents said it is fine to call me at home

(Continued on page 172.)

about the letter of recommendation as well. Our home number is 606–555–9299.

Thank you in advance for your consideration.

Respectfully yours,

Alexis Young

Alexis Young

USEFUL WORDS AND PHRASES

Thank you in advance for your consideration.

✳

I am writing to request a letter of recommendation for me for [college or institution].

✳

Please let me know if there are any details you would like me to provide in advance.

✳

I am hoping I can request...

✳

I hope that you will be able to...

✳

Respectfully yours,

✳

Sincerely yours,

WRITING LETTERS OF RECOMMENDATION

Being asked to write a recommendation letter for a current or former student, employee, or even an acquaintance is considered an honor to some. The requestor is trusting you enough to write a positive assessment of his or her character, academic experience, or work ethic that could very well change their life, help them get into a college of their choice, or help them land a job.

Letters of recommendation should be short and sincere and should only discuss the qualities of the person that are relevant. For example, if you're a teacher and writing a letter of recommendation to a college for a student, write about why this candidate is an exceptional student or leader in the classroom. Specifically state why you are recommending the person and which school the recommendation is for so that the letter is tailored to the specific institution.

A successful letter of recommendation sets the candidate apart from the hundreds or even thousands of candidates vying for one of those spots. Organizational skills, leadership skills, and the ability to problem solve or think critically are all things to consider addressing. Do not be afraid to give a short but specific and concrete example of one of these qualities. At the end of the letter, thank the reader for their time and offer a way that you can be best contacted if they wish to speak to you directly. Finally, use a complimentary close followed by your signature and title. In some cases, you will also need to sign across the seal on the back of the sealed envelope to prove that the letter has not been tampered with.

Letter of Recommendation

Sam Priebe
Physics Department
Bellinghamton Senior High School
351 Lincoln Road
Bellinghamton, WI 53562

November 14, 2014

Northeastern University
Application Processing Center
P.O. Box 120
Randolph, MA 02368–9998

Dear Admissions Officers,

In addition to completing the information required for teacher evaluation on the Common Application, I am including this statement about Alexis Young, a candidate for admissions at Northeastern University.

I had the pleasure of teaching Alexis in Physics I during her junior year at Bellinghamton Senior High School. In my 25 years of experience as a Physics teacher, I have rarely found a student who has a thirst for knowledge like Alexis. Her dedication to her work, even when challenged, is one that not only makes her a student, but also a scholar. Her attention to detail, passion for research, and overall sense of disciplined determination are qualities that will make her an asset to whatever program of study she sets her sights on.

Though Alexis is able to follow instructions and follow through with complex analysis, she is not a follower, but a leader in every sense of the word. Alexis possesses an infectious enthusiasm for whatever she is involved in. She has excelled in all of her courses, and unlike many students who take to the sciences, she is quite outspoken and vibrant. Alexis is so organized that she presented me with a letter to request a letter of recommendation for her at the start of the school year. It is that kind of maturity and responsibility, along with her academic and social achievements at Bellinghamton, that make her ready for collegiate study, and she will be an asset to your university.

If you wish to speak to me directly about Ms. Young, I can be reached at 606–555–2300.

Thank you for the opportunity to recommend such a stellar student.

Very sincerely yours,

Mr. Samuel Priebe

Mr. Samuel Priebe

Professional Letter of Recommendation

Sam Alicea
675 Lakeshore Drive
Chicago, IL 60611

August 5, 2013

Mr. Lloyd J. Manning, CEO
Thinktank Associates
5000 Industrial Way
Jackson, MS 39204

Re: Letter of Recommendation for Peter Sampson

Dear Mr. Manning:

I understand that Peter Sampson has applied for a position with Thinktank Associates. Peter and I worked together for seven years on several projects with The Other Big Thinktank. I retired from the company three years ago and throughout my relationship with Peter, I cannot say that I have met or worked with a finer person. His tenacity and problem solving skills are phenomenal and he has a gift for thinking "out of the box" in order to maximize the potential for R&D projects.

As I am sure you already know, he has several publications under his belt and as such, has proven strong research skills and an ability to communicate them well to his colleagues not only in writing, but in person as well.

I highly recommend Peter for the position of Director of Research and Development at Thinktank Associates.

I have watched him blossom in his career, and the time is ripe for him to take on new challenges and have the chance to truly put his leadership skills to good use.

If you have any questions or wish to speak with me about Peter directly, I am more than happy to do so. Please do not hesitate to call. I can be reached at (724) 555–9784 anytime that is convenient for you.

Very sincerely yours,

Sam Alicea

Sam Alicea

USEFUL WORDS AND PHRASES

I am recommending ____ because he/she...

✳

____ would be an asset to your institution because...

✳

I had the joy to work with ____ while...

✳

After ____ years of service,

✳

____ is a true leader because...

✳

____ is an outstanding example of academic excellence.

✷ Chapter 17 ✷
E-mail

Even with the presence of postal and interoffice mail, most of us use e-mail as our predominant way of communicating with friends, family, and coworkers. Because we have come to rely so much on electronic communication, we are more apt to quickly type something and hit send—often without spell checking and proofreading. In general, though, the same rules that apply to traditional correspondence also apply to electronic communication. In this chapter, we'll discuss some of the intricacies of e-mail, and give tips and cautions that you may find useful.

E-MAIL FORMAT

The format of electronic mail (e-mail) takes on the traditional written-memo format. Some portions of an e-mail are automatic; others you can configure so they are automatically included, such as your signature. However, you should follow the same conventions when composing an e-mail that you would when writing on paper.

THE ANATOMY OF E-MAIL

All e-mail, regardless of which service provider you use, includes the following fields:

* To:
* From:

* Subject:
* Body:

All service providers automatically stamp an e-mail with its date and time, so you don't need to configure those fields.

THE AUTOMATIC FIELDS

The "To:" field should have the e-mail address of the recipient. The "From:" field is your e-mail address and is automatically filled in when you compose or reply to an e-mail. The "Subject:" field (or "Re:" field) is what the e-mail is about. Always remember to fill in this field. In this Internet age of spam and online advertisements, more and more people mistake a blank subject line for junk mail, even if the sender's e-mail address is a familiar one. If you want your e-mail to be read, avoid sending messages with a blank subject field. Keep the text in the subject field short and to the point. It's a good idea to refrain from using generic subject lines, such as "hello," "hi," and other similar phrases, as these can also suggest the message is spam. To avoid your message being treated as spam by either the e-mail program or the recipient, be more specific when titling your subject.

THE BODY

Follow the conventions of standard letter writing in the body of an e-mail. For personal e-mail, start with "Dear" and the recipient's name. If you do not know the person well or are writing for business purposes, use their title and surname.

Write in short, clear sentences and keep the e-mail as brief and to the point as possible. Keep paragraphs short, so that your reader is not overwhelmed by a block of text on their screen. If you are including attachments, inform the recipient that attachments are included with a brief explanation of what they contain, if necessary. Be aware of the size of the attachments you are sending, as some internet service providers have limits on the size of attachments that can be received.

When composing an e-mail, use standard language instead of slipping into Internet shorthand, especially in business e-mail. "'Net speak" is too informal and not everyone who uses e-mail is familiar with the shorthand reserved for chat rooms, instant messaging, and Internet forums. To be a cyber savvy e-mailer, you need to be able to know when to use casual or formal language.

End the note with a complimentary close and your signature.

THE SIGNATURE LINE

Most e-mail providers allow you to set a standard signature that is automatically included at the end of every message. Your signature should not be complicated, but at the very least, it should contain your name. Your signature will probably vary depending on whether the e-mail is personal or for business. When sending a personal e-mail, using only your first name is acceptable. You could also include any other personal information such as your telephone numbers, URL of your personal Web site, or even a favorite quote.

When sending business e-mail, regardless of whether the e-mail address you're using is your official work e-mail address or your personal e-mail, you want to be professional. Your business signature should include your first and last names, title, company name, your business telephone numbers, and the URL of the company Web site. You can also include your personal cell phone number if you need to be reached for business matters while out of the office. Unless other information directly relates to your business, do not include it in your business e-mail signature.

OTHER E-MAIL FEATURES

Carbon Copy

The Carbon Copy (CC) and Blind Carbon Copy (BCC) fields are where you place the e-mail addresses of anyone else you wish to see the e-mail besides the actual recipient. The "CC:" field is for when you want the direct recipient to be aware of who else is receiving the message. The "BCC:" field is for when you don't want the recipient to know who else is receiving the message. The "BCC:" field can also be used when you're sending the same e-mail to several people, such as in a newsletter to family and friends, and you want to protect each recipient's privacy, since all addresses placed in the "To:" and "CC:" fields will appear in every recipient's e-mail.

Priority

Some e-mail providers let you set the level of priority for an e-mail as low, standard, or high. Others also allow you to receive a return receipt, which will notify you when a recipient has received and opened your e-mail.

The priority feature should be used sparingly. In other words, do not set all of your e-mails as "high priority" unless it is extremely important that the recipient read and/or respond to your e-mail as soon as possible. Also remember that some service providers do not recognize the return-receipt feature, so even if you have set your e-mail to send you a return receipt, you may not get one.

DON'T HIT "SEND" YET

Before you hit "send," reread your e-mail and proofread it using your e-mail program's spell-check feature. If the e-mail is business-related or contains important information, it's a good idea to print it out to proofread it before sending. Spell check will not catch every typo and error. Remember that if you typed "hat" and meant to type "hit," spell check will not catch the error since both words are real words. That may not be a huge blunder when sending e-mail to friends and family, but if you were sending a business e-mail about how well last night's fundraiser was and wrote, "the fundraiser was a big hat," you won't come off well.

Double-check any dates against a calendar. Make sure that if you give both a day and a date for an event or appointment (for example, Thursday the 7th), that the 7th is indeed on a Thursday.

Another reason to pause before hitting "send" is if you are sending an angry, private, or intimate e-mail. You can save the e-mail as a draft to send out later, sleep on it for a day or two, and reopen it to make any necessary edits before sending.

PERSONAL E-MAIL, GROUP E-MAIL, AND PRIVACY

E-mail, like any other form of written communication, assumes a certain level of privacy between the correspondents. However, its privacy is not as infallible as one might think. Written letters can be burned, shredded, or flushed down the toilet. E-mail cannot. E-mail can be traced, computer keystrokes can be recorded, and communications records are maintained by your provider. Those are other reasons to pause before hitting "send," especially if you are using your work e-mail account at your employer's expense or are sending personal, sensitive, or intimate information.

Avoid using your work e-mail for personal business. In fact, it is often a violation of company policy for many businesses. This includes using work computers to check personal e-mail accounts. Not all companies enforce this rule, but it is a good rule to live by as a professional.

When you write a business e-mail, assume that it may be forwarded to others at your company, or at your contact's company, to pass along information or to keep someone updated on a project.

When sending a carbon copy of an e-mail and for any group e-mail, you can assume that any sense of privacy is gone now that more than two people are privy to the exchanged information. If the e-mail is of a sensitive nature, consider who should receive it and only send it to that person or people. You can send group e-mail by inserting all the recipients' e-mail addresses in the "To:" field, "CC:" field, or "BCC:" field. Using the last method to send a group an e-mail is beneficial when you do not want to share their e-mail addresses with everyone else on the list. The "BCC:" field is also a good method to use since many spam filters are set to catch bulk and group e-mails with many e-mail addresses in the "To:" field. This might ensure that a legitimate group e-mail gets through.

When replying to a group message, make sure you hit "reply" instead of "reply to all" unless you know every single person on the list and your response is one that every person needs to read.

TIPS

Do

* include a subject line.

* check the "To" field to make sure you're sending your message only to the intended people.

* reread your e-mail and use spell check before sending it.

* be brief and succinct.

* use the BCC field to send an e-mail to large groups of people.

Don't

* use the "high priority" setting for all your messages.

* use your work e-mail for personal business.

* include attachments that will be too large for the recipient's mailbox.

* use all capital letters for emphasis. It comes across as shouting.

⇒ Chapter 18 ⇐

Texting and Social Media

If you're hesitant to start using some of the newer forms of communication, we've got some tips and hints for you, as you branch out into texting, Facebook, Twitter, and LinkedIn.

TEXTING

It seems like just about everyone, from preteens to octogenarians, has a cell phone. But if you're only using your phone to make calls, you're missing out on a very useful feature: text messaging. While it can certainly be nice to call friends and family members and engage in lengthy conversation, sometimes our busy lives get in the way and there just isn't enough time. Or, we'll play a frustrating game of "phone tag," calling back and forth but never actually reaching a person. And what about the people who loudly answer phone calls in the middle of a nice restaurant or a movie theater? While it is understandable that someone may need to reach you at times like these, you never want to come across as the rude person who interrupts other diners.

Texting addresses all of these issues. With text messages, you can send friends or family members a message, and they can reply at their leisure. You can still engage in conversations, but the conversation unfolds at the pace of each person, so no one feels rushed or bothered. Texting is also a great way to end "phone tag"—simply text a message to the person who tried to call, and include a time when you will be available to talk. That way, you can both decide on a time that will work for each of you. And if you do receive a call in the middle of dinner or a movie, you can text the caller to ask about the importance of the call. If it's urgent, simply excuse yourself and find a place to make the call where it will not be bothersome to other patrons.

As with social media, you should use your best judgment about when it is appropriate to send text messages as opposed to sending written correspondence. While your best friend may not mind a text message "thank you" for treating you to lunch, chances are there are many people who still expect handwritten thank-you notes for gifts or the occasional personal note in a birthday card. But for casual conversations, text messages are a great tool.

Sending a text message is easier than you might think. Most smart phones have full keyboards that make typing out a message simple and self-explanatory—although you do want to make sure that any autofill or autocomplete features do not result in an accidental change to your message. After that, it's just a matter of choosing a contact and hitting "send." Messages are usually limited to about 160 characters, although if your text ends up being longer than that, your phone will automatically send multiple messages. But if you don't have a phone plan that allows unlimited text messages, you'll probably want to keep your messages short. With text messages, it is perfectly acceptable to use shortcuts—it is not uncommon to see words abbreviated, or to even use "u" in place of "you," or "ur" in place of "you're" or "your."

As with any new technology, the best way to learn about text messaging is to just start texting. Before long, it'll be NP to send messages, and you'll LOL at how easy it is. KWIM?*

SOCIAL MEDIA

One of the most popular ways to keep in touch in the modern world is with the help of social media. Social media includes well-known websites such as Facebook, Twitter, and LinkedIn. While they may seem intimidating at first glance, once you get the hang of them these sites can be useful, convenient, and fun.

Before you begin participating in the world of social media, you'll need to decide on a username and a password. Your password should not be anything that would be easy for other people to guess—try to avoid names, birth dates, or any other easily accessible information. And don't forget to write it down and keep it in a safe place, in case you forget it. Once you have a profile on any of these sites, you can begin to add contacts. Chances are, you already know many people who use social media, so be sure that the people you add to your contact lists are people you know or are acquainted with in some way.

One of the best ways to get used to these websites is to just jump right in and start looking around—you might be confused at first, but before you know it, you'll be familiar with all of the features and discover that they're easier to use than you may have thought!

Communication by social media tends to be informal. As always when you write, however, keep in mind both your

---

*NP = no problem. LOL = Laugh out loud. KWIM = Know what I mean?

intended audience and whether your message might reach further than your intended audience. Don't post in anger or haste, and take the time to reread before you click the "Send," "Post," or "Update" button.

Facebook

Once you have a Facebook profile, you can customize it in many different ways. Familiarize yourself with the website's privacy settings, so you know who is able to access your information, and then add as much or as little personal information to your profile as you'd like.

Facebook is very versatile, so it's a great way to keep friends and family up-to-date with what's going on in your life without having to individually contact each person. You'll notice a "status" box at the top of your profile page. This is where you can share pretty much whatever you'd like—what you ate for breakfast, your thoughts on the latest best-selling novel, opinions on your favorite sports team—the sky's the limit.

You can also post links to online articles, blogs, websites, or whatever you find interesting. Your contacts (or "friends" as they're called in the world of Facebook) can then leave you comments, and you in turn can leave comments on any of their pages. So even if you live in Miami and your sister lives in Seattle, you can still swap stories about your kids, share recipes, exchange photographs, or talk about the weather every day.

Facebook can also be used to invite people to events, especially less formal events. Some people set up a Facebook event in conjunction with invitations sent in the mail, to ask people to "Save the date" before invitations are sent out, to allow for easier reply, and to ensure that people who might misplace the invitation can always check on the event details.

Keep an eye on your posting settings. You may want to post something that the public can see, something that only your contacts can see, or something that only a subset of your contacts can see. Facebook also has a tab labeled "messages," which is where you can privately send messages to one or more of your contacts. PMs, or private messages, can be a good way to arrange meetings or check in on something quickly.

Especially if you have work colleagues or people you don't know very well on your Facebook feed, it's best to maintain proper grammar and punctuation when posting to Facebook. Be wise about the kinds of things you say and the pictures you share. Nowadays, it is not uncommon for employers to search for prospective employees on the internet, to see what sort of information pops up. So it's best to keep the crazy party pictures off of Facebook, and to save the angry political diatribes for another time.

Be careful also about sharing information that may not be widely known yet—if you hear about an engagement or pregnancy, for example, don't speak about it on Facebook unless the people involved have given their permission. And be mindful of those comments you post on the pages of your contacts—remember that your audience may include their relatives and colleagues.

Twitter

Twitter is considered a "microblogging" website. This means that the postings must be short, concise, and to-the-point. Unlike Facebook, Twitter allows only 140 characters per post, or "tweet." Because of this limit, you can be a bit more lax with your grammar, spelling, and punctuation usage. It can be difficult to write complete sentences and manage to convey a coherent point with 140 characters, so with Twitter, it's more acceptable to take shortcuts.

Twitter is useful for sharing quick thoughts and ideas, and has become quite popular even as a business tool. One of the unique features of Twitter is the "hashtag," which is a pound sign (#) followed by a word or phrase with no spaces or punctuation. Think of a hashtag as the keyword or main topic of a Tweet. Users can search for the topics they're interested in, and find all of the Tweets with the same hashtag. Hashtags should be used sparingly—usually no more than two per Tweet—to avoid cluttering up your message.

It is common for people to "retweet" messages, sharing them with their own Twitter feed. When you post, always remember that your tweet may travel much further and be seen by many more people than you originally intended.

LinkedIn

LinkedIn has been called "Facebook for professionals." It has a similar set-up as other social media sites—you create a profile and add contacts—but LinkedIn is specifically used for business-related purposes. So instead of telling your contacts about your love of action movies or Jane Austen novels, you can post your resume, work experience, and business-related interests.

Your contacts on LinkedIn provide you with a "network" of like-minded professionals. This can be especially useful if you feel that you're stuck in an unfulfilling job or are worried about a sudden layoff. Having a network of professional contacts assures that you can be aware of new job prospects, and gives you the ability to see what sorts of companies are hiring. It is a far cry from the days of searching through "want ads" in the newspaper—and much more efficient!

Since LinkedIn is a professional networking site, all of your communications should be as polished and articulate as possible. After all, your profile may be the first impression a prospective employer has of you.

Social media has changed the way we communicate—not only personally, but professionally, as well. While websites like Facebook and Twitter are great for casual communication, you should use good judgment when deciding whether to use them in place of written correspondence. But since social media is no doubt here to stay, don't be afraid to embrace the new changes and discover how useful it can be!